Sara Jeannette Duncan

His Honour and a lady

By Mrs. Everard Cotes

Sara Jeannette Duncan

His Honour and a lady
By Mrs. Everard Cotes

ISBN/EAN: 9783337107765

Printed in Europe, USA, Canada, Australia, Japan

Cover: Foto ©ninafisch / pixelio.de

More available books at **www.hansebooks.com**

HIS HONOUR, AND A LADY

BY

MRS. EVERARD COTES
(SARA JEANNETTE DUNCAN)

AUTHOR OF A SOCIAL DEPARTURE, AN AMERICAN GIRL IN LONDON,
A DAUGHTER OF TO-DAY, VERNON'S AUNT,
THE STORY OF SONNY SAHIB, ETC.

NEW YORK
D. APPLETON AND COMPANY
1896

COPYRIGHT, 1895, 1896,
BY D. APPLETON AND COMPANY.

LIST OF ILLUSTRATIONS.

	FACING PAGE
The situation made its voiceless demand	*Frontispiece*
"She seems to be sufficiently entertained"	21
There was a moment's pause	83
Notwithstanding, it was gay enough	150
"What do I know about the speech"!	215
She drove back	305

HIS HONOUR, AND A LADY.

CHAPTER I.

"THE Sahib *walks!*" said Ram Prasannad, who dusted the office books and papers, to Bundal Singh the messenger, who wore a long red coat with a badge of office, and went about the business of the Queen-Empress on his two lean brown legs.

"What talk is that?" Bundal Singh shifted his betel quid to the other cheek and lunged upon his feet. This in itself was something. When one sits habitually upon one's heels the process of getting up is not undertaken lightly. The men looked out together between the whitewashed stucco pillars of the long verandah that interposed between the Commissioner's clerks and the glare and publicity of the outer world of Hassimabad. Overhead, in a pipal tree that threw sharp-cut patterns of its heart-shaped leaves about their feet, a crow stretched its grey-black throat in strenuous caws, since it was ten o'clock in the morning and there was no reason to keep silence. Farther away a chorus of other crows smote the sunlight, and from the direction of the bazar came a murmur of the life there, borne higher now and then in the wailing voice of some hawker of sweetmeats. Nevertheless there was a boundless stillness, a stillness that might have been commanded. The prodigal sun intensified it, and the trees stood in it, a red and dusty road wound through it, and the figure of a man, walking quickly down the road, seemed to be a concentration of it.

"That signifies," continued Ram Prasannad, without emotion, "news that is either very good or very bad. The Government *lát* had but arrived, the sahib opened one letter only—which is now with him—and in a breath he was gone, walking, though the horse was still fast between the shafts. Myself, I think the news is good, for my cousin—he is a writing baboo in the Home

Office, dost thou understand, thou, runner of errands!—has sent word to me that the sahib is much in favour with the *Burra Lat*, and that it would be well to be faithful to him."

"I will go swiftly after with an umbrella, and from his countenance it will appear," remarked Bundal Singh; "and look thou, worthy one, if that son of mud, Lal Beg, the grain dealer, comes again in my absence to try to make petition to the sahib, and brings a pice less than one rupee to me, do thou refuse him admission."

Bundal Singh ran after his master, as he said. As John Church walked rapidly, and the habitual pace of a Queen's messenger in red and gold is a dignified walk, the umbrella was tendered with a devoted loss of wind.

"It may be that your honour will take harm from the sun," Bundal Singh suggested, with the privilege all the Commissioner's people felt permitted to use. The Commissioner liked it— could be depended upon to appreciate any little savour of personal devotion to him, even if it took the form of a liberty. He had not a servant who was unaware of this or failed to presume upon it, in his place and degree. This one got a nod of acknowledgment as his master took the opened umbrella, and observed, as he fell behind, that the sahib was too much preoccupied to carry it straight. He went meditatively back to Ram Prasannad in the verandah, who said, "Well?"

"Simply it does not appear. The sahib's forehead had twenty wrinkles, and his mind was a thousand miles hence. Yet it was as if he had lately smiled and would smile again. What will be, will be. Lal Beg has not been here?"

John Church walked steadily on, with his near-sighted eyes fixed always upon the wide space of sunlit road, its red dust thick-printed with bare feet and hoofs, that lay in front of him—seeing nothing, literally, but the way home. He met no one who knew him except people from the bazar, who regarded their vizier with serious wonder as they salaamed, the men who sat upon low bamboo carts and urged, hand upon flank, the peaceful-eyed cattle yoked to them, turning to stare as they jogged indolently past.

A brown pariah, curled up in the middle of the road, lifted his long snout in lazy apology as Church stepped round him, trusting the sense that told him it would not be necessary to get out of the way. As he passed the last low wall, mossy and discoloured, that divided its brilliantly tangled garden from the highway, and turned in at its own gate, he caught himself out of his abstraction and threw up his head. He entered his wife's drawing-room considerately, and a ray of light, slipping through the curtains and past the azaleas and across the cool duskness of the place, fell on his spectacles and exaggerated the triumph in his face.

The lady, who sat at the other end of the room writing, rose as her husband came into it, and stepped forward softly to meet him. If you had known her you would have noticed a slight elation in her step that was not usual, and made it more graceful, if anything, than it commonly was.

"I think I know what you have come to tell me," she said. Her voice matched her personality so perfectly that it might have suggested her, to a few people, in her darkened drawing-room, as its perfume would betray some sweet-smelling thing in the evening. Not to John Church. "I think I know," she said, as he hesitated for words that would not show extravagant or undignified gratification. "But tell me yourself. It will be a pleasure."

"That Sir Griffiths Spence goes on eighteen months' sick leave, and——"

"And that you are appointed to officiate for him. Yes."

"Somebody has written?"

"Yes—Mr. Ancram."

His wife had come close to him, and he noticed that she was holding out her hands in her impulse of congratulation. He took one of them—it was all he felt the occasion required—and shook it lamely. She dropped the other with a little quick turn of her head and a dash of amusement at her own expense in the gentle gravity of her expression. "Do sit down," she said, almost as if he had been a visitor, "and tell me all about it." She dragged a comfortable chair forward out of its relation with a Burmese carved table, some pots of ferns and a screen, and sat down herself opposite, leaning forward in a little pose of expectancy. Church placed himself on the edge of it, grasping his hat with both hands between his knees.

"I must apologise for my boots," he said, looking down: "I walked over. I am very dusty."

"What does it matter? You are King of Bengal!"

"Acting King."

"It is the same thing—or it will be. Sir Griffiths retires altogether in two years—Lord Scansleigh evidently intends you to succeed him." The lady spoke with obvious repression, but her gray eyes and the warm whiteness of her oval face seemed to have caught into themselves all the light and shadow of the room.

"Perhaps—perhaps. You always invest in the future at a premium, Judith. I don't intend to think about that."

Such an anticipation, based on his own worth, seemed to him unwarrantable, almost indecent.

"I do," she said, wilfully ignoring the clouding of his face. "There is so much to think about. First the pay—almost ten thousand rupees a month—and we are poor. It may be a material consideration, but I don't mind confessing that the prospect of never having to cut the khansamah appeals to me. We shall have a palace and a park to live in, with a guard at the gates, and two outriders with swords to follow our carriage. We shall live in Calcutta, where there are trams and theatres and shops and people. The place carries knighthood if you are confirmed in it, and you will be Sir John Church—that gratifies the snob that is latent in me because I am a woman, John." (She paused and glanced at his face, which had grown almost morose.) "Best of all," she added lightly, "as Lieutenant-Governor of Bengal you will be practically sole ruler of eighty millions of people. You will be free to carry out your own theories, and to undertake reforms—any number of reforms! Mr. Ancram says," she went on, after a moment's hesitation, "that the man and the opportunity have come together."

John Church blushed, through his beard

which was gray, and over the top of his head which was bald, but his look lightened.

"Ancram will be one of my secretaries," he said. "Does he speak at all—does he mention the way it has been taken in Calcutta?"

Mrs. Church went to her writing-table and came back with the letter. It was luxuriously written, in a rapid hand as full of curves and angles as a woman's, and covered, from "Dear Lady" to "Always yours sincerely," several broad-margined sheets.

"I think he does," she said, deliberately searching the pages. "Yes: 'Church was not thought precisely in the running—you are so remote in Hassimabad, and his work has always been so unostentatious—and there was some surprise when the news came, but no cavil. It is known that the Viceroy has been looking almost with tears for a man who would be strong enough to redeem a few of Sir Griffiths' mistakes if possible while he is away—he has been, as you know, ludicrously weak with the natives —and Church's handling of that religious uproar you had a year ago has not been forgotten. I need not expatiate upon the pleasure your friends feel, but it may gratify you to know that the official mob is less ready with criticism of His Excellency's choice than usual.'"

John Church listened with the look of putting his satisfaction under constraint. He listened in the official manner, as one who has many things to hear, with his head bent forward and toward his wife, and his eyes consideringly upon the floor.

"I am glad of that," he said nervously when she had finished—" I am glad of that. There is a great deal to be done in Bengal, and matters will be simplified if they recognise it."

"I think you would find a great deal to do anywhere, John," remarked Mrs. Church. It could almost be said that she spoke kindly, and a sensitive observer with a proper estimate of her husband might have found this irritating. During the little while that followed, however, as they talked, in the warmth of this unexpected gratification, of what his work had been as a Commissioner, and what it might be as a Lieutenant-Governor, it would have been evident even to an observer who was not sensitive, that here they touched a high-water mark of their intercourse, a climax in the cordiality of their mutual understanding.

"By the way," said John Church, getting up to go, "when is Ancram to be married?"

"I don't know!" Mrs. Church threw some interest into the words. Her inflection said that she was surprised that she didn't know. "He only mentions Miss Daye to call her a 'study in femininity,' which looks as if he might be submitting to a protracted process of education at her hands. Certainly not soon, I should think."

"Ancram must be close on forty, with good pay, good position, good prospects. He shouldn't put it off any longer: a man has no business to grow old alone in this country. He deteriorates."

Church pulled himself together with a shake—he was a loose-hung creature—and put a nervous hand up to his necktie. Then he pulled down his cuffs, considered his hat with the effect of making quite sure that there was nothing more to say, and turned to go.

"You might send me over something," he said, glancing at his watch. "I won't be able to come back to breakfast. Already I've lost three-quarters of an hour from work. Government doesn't pay me for that. You are pleased, then?" he added, looking round at her in a half shamefaced way from the door.

Mrs. Church had returned to the writing-table, and had again taken up her pen. She leaned back in her chair and lifted her delicate chin with a smile that had custom and patience in it.

"Very pleased indeed," she said; and he went away. The intelligent observer, again, would have wondered how he refrained from going back and kissing her. Perhaps the custom and the patience in her smile would have lent themselves to the explanation. At all events, he went away.

He was forty-two, exactly double her age, when he married Judith Strange, eight years before, in Stoneborough, a small manufacturing town in the north of England, where her father was a Nonconformist minister. He was her opportunity, and she had taken him, with private congratulation that she could respect him and private qualms as to whether her respect was her crucial test of him—considered in the light of an opportunity. Not in any sordid sense; she would be more inclined perhaps to apologise for herself than I am to apologise for her. But with an inordinately hungry capacity for life she had the narrowest conditions to live in. She knew by intuition that the world was full of colour and passion, and when one is tormented with this sort of knowledge it becomes more than ever grievous to inhabit one of its small, dull, grimy blind alleys, with the single anticipation of enduring to a smoke-blackened old age, like one of Stoneborough's lesser chimneys. There was nothing ideal about John Church except his honesty,—already he stooped, already he was grey, sallow and serious, with the slenderest interest in questions that could not express their utility in unquestionable facts, —but when he asked her to marry him, the wall at the end of the alley fell down, and a breeze stole in from the far East, with a vision of palms and pomegranates. She accepted him for the sake of her imagination, wishing profoundly that he was not so much like her father, with what her mother thought almost improper promptitude; and for a long time, although he still stood outside it, her imagination loyally rewarded her. She felt the East to her fingertips, and her mere physical life there became a thing of vivid experience, to be valued for itself. If her husband confounded this joy in her expansion with the orthodox happiness of a devoted wife, it cannot be said that he was particularly to blame for his mistake, for numbers of other people made it also. And when, after eight years of his companionship, and that of the sunburned policeman, the anæmic magistrate, the agreeable doctor, their wives, the odd colonel, and the stray subalterns that constituted society in the stations they lived in, she began to show a little lassitude of spirit, he put it down not unnaturally to the climate, and wished he could conscientiously take a few months' leave, since nothing would induce her to go to England without him. By this time India had become a resource, India that lay all about her, glowing, profuse, mysterious, fascinating, a place in which she felt that she had no part, could never have any part, but that of a spectator. The gesture of a fakir, the red masses of the gold-mohur trees against the blue intensity of the sky, the heavy sweetness of the evening wind, the soft colour and curves of the homeward driven cattle, the little naked babies with their jingling anklets in the bazar—she had begun to turn to these things seeking their gift of pleasure jealously, consciously thankful that, in spite of the Amusement Club, she could never be altogether bored.

John Church went back to work with his satisfaction sweetened by the fact that his wife had told him that she was very pleased indeed, while Mrs. Church answered the Honourable Mr. Lewis Ancram's letter.

"I have been making my own acquaintance this morning," she said among other things, "as an ambitious woman. It is intoxicating, after this idle, sun-filled, wondering life, with the single supreme care that John does not wear ragged collars to church—as a Commissioner he ought to be extravagant in collars—to be confronted with something to assume and carry out, a part to play, with all India looking on. Don't imagine a lofty intention on my part to inspire my husband's Resolutions. I assure you I see myself differently. Perhaps, after all, it is the foolish anticipation of my state and splendour that has excited my vain imagination as much as anything. Already, prospectively, I murmur lame nothings into the ear of the Viceroy as he takes me down to dinner! But I am preposterously delighted. To-morrow is Sunday—I have an irreverent desire for the prayers of all the churches."

CHAPTER II.

"HERE you are at last!" remarked Mrs. Daye with vivacity, taking the three long, pronounced and rustling steps which she took so very well, toward the last comer to her dinner party, who made his leisurely entrance between the *portières*, pocketing his handkerchief. "Don't say you have been to church," she went on, holding out a condoning hand, "for none of us will believe you."

Although Mr. Ancram's lips curved back over his rather prominent teeth in a narrow smile as he put up his eyeglass and looked down at his hostess, Mrs. Daye felt the levity fade out of her expression: she had to put compulsion on herself to keep it in her face. It was as if she, his prospective mother-in-law, had taken the least of liberties with Mr. Ancram.

"Does the only road to forgiveness lie

through the church gate?" he asked. His voice was high and agreeable; it expressed discrimination; his tone implied that, if the occasion had required it, he could have said something much cleverer easily—an implication no one who knew him would have found unwarrantable.

"The padres say it does, as a rule, Ancram," put in Colonel Daye. "In this case it lies through the dining-room door. Will you take my wife in?"

In a corner of the room, which she might have chosen for its warm obscurity, Rhoda Daye watched with curious scrutiny the lightest detail of Mr. Lewis Ancram's behaviour. An elderly gentleman, with pulpy red cheeks and an amplitude of white waistcoat, stood beside her chair, swaying out of the perpendicular with well-bred rigidity now and then, in tentative efforts at conversation; to which she replied, "Really?" and "Yes, I know," while her eyes fixed themselves upon Ancram's face, and her little white features gleamed immobile under the halo which the tall lamp behind her made with her fuzz of light-brown hair. "Mother's respect for him is simply outrageous," she reflected, as she assured the elderly gentleman that even for Calcutta the heat was really extraordinary, considering that they were in December. "I wonder—supposing he had not made love to me—if I could have had as much!" She did not answer herself definitely—not from any lack of candour, but because the question presented difficulties. She slipped past him presently on the arm of the elderly gentleman, as Ancram still stood with bent head talking to her mother. His eyes sought hers with a significance that flattered her—there was no time for further greeting—and the bow with which he returned her enigmatic little nod singled her out for consideration. As she went in to dinner the nape of Mr. Lewis Ancram's neck and the parting of his hair remained with her as pictorial facts.

Mrs. Daye always gave composite dinner-parties, and this was one of them. "If you ask nobody but military people to meet each other," she was in the habit of saying, "you hear nothing but the price of chargers and the prospects of the Staff Corps. If you make your list up of civilians, the conversation consists of abuse of their official superiors and the infamous conduct of the Secretary of State about the rupee." On this occasion Mrs. Daye had reason to anticipate that the price of chargers would be varied by the grievances of the Civil Service, and that a touring Member of Parliament would participate in the discussion who knew nothing about either; and she felt that her blend would be successful. She could give herself up to the somewhat fearful enjoyment she experienced in Mr. Ancram's society. Mrs. Daye was convinced that nobody appreciated Mr. Ancram more subtly than she did. She saw a great deal of jealousy of him in Calcutta society, whereas she was wont to declare that, for her part, she found nothing extraordinary in the way he had got in—a man of his brains, you know! And if Calcutta resented this imputation upon its own brains in ever so slight a degree, Mrs. Daye saw therein more jealousy of the fact that her family circle was about to receive him. When it had once opened for that purpose and closed again, Mrs. Daye hoped vaguely that she would be sus-

tained for the new and exacting duty of living up to Mr. Ancram.

"*Please* look at Rhoda," she begged, in a conversational buzz that her blend had induced.

Mr. Ancram looked, deliberately, but with appreciation. "She seems to be sufficiently entertained," he said.

"Oh, she is! She's got a globe-trotter. Haven't you found out that Rhoda simply loves globe-trotters? She declares that she renews her youth in them."

" Her first impressions, I suppose she means?"

" Oh, as to what she *means*——"

Mrs. Daye broke off irresolutely, and thoughtfully conveyed a minute piece of roll to her lips. The minute piece of roll was Mr. Ancram's opportunity to complete Mrs. Daye's suggestion of a certain interesting ambiguity in her daughter; but he did not take it. He continued to look attentively at Miss Daye, who appeared, as he said, to be sufficiently entertained, under circumstances which seemed to him inadequate. Her traveller was talking emphatically, with gestures of elderly dogmatism, and she was deferentially listening, an amusement behind her eyes with which the Chief Secretary to the Government at Bengal was not altogether unfamiliar. He had seen it there before, on occasions when there was apparently nothing to explain it.

"It would be satisfactory to see her eating her dinner," he remarked, with what Mrs. Daye felt to be too slight a degree of solicitude. She was obliged to remind herself that at thirty-seven a man was apt to take these things more as matters of fact, especially—and there was a double comfort in this reflection—a man already well up in the Secretariat and known to be ambitious. "Is it possible," Mr. Ancram went on, somewhat absently, "that these are Calcutta roses? You must have a very clever gardener."

"No"—and Mrs. Daye pitched her voice with a gentle definiteness that made what she was saying interesting all round the table—"they came from the Viceroy's place at Barrackpore. Lady Emily sent them to me: so sweet of her, I thought! I always think it particularly kind when people in that position trouble themselves about one; they must have so *many* demands upon their time."

The effect could not have been better. Everybody looked at the roses with an interest that might almost be described as respectful; and Mrs. Delaine, whose husband was Captain Delaine of the Durham Rifles, said that she would have known them for Their Excellencies' roses anywhere—they always did the table with that kind for the Thursday dinners at Government House—she had never known them to use any other.

Mrs. St. George, whose husband was the Presidency Magistrate, found this interesting. "Do they really?" she exclaimed. "I've often wondered what those big Thursday affairs were like. Fancy—we've been in Calcutta through three cold weathers now, and have never been asked to anything but little private dinners at Government House—not more than eight or ten, you know!"

"Don't you prefer that?" asked Mrs. Delaine, taking her quenching with noble equanimity.

"Well, of course one sees more *of* them," Mrs. St. George admitted. "The last time we were there, about a fortnight ago, I had a long chat with Lady Emily. She is a sweet thing, and perfectly wild at being out of the school-room!" Mrs. St. George added that it was a charming family, so well brought up; and this seemed to be a matter of special congratulation as affecting the domestic arrangements of a Viceroy. There was a warmth and an emphasis in the corroboration that arose which almost established relations of intimacy between Their Excellencies and Mrs. Daye's dinner-party. Mrs. Daye's daughter listened in her absorbed, noting manner; and when the elderly gentleman remarked with a certain solemnity that they were talking of the Scansleighs, he supposed, the smile with which she said "Evidently" was more pronounced than he could have had any right to expect.

"They seem to be delightful people," continued the elderly gentleman, earnestly.

"I daresay," Miss Daye replied, with grave deliberation. "They're very decorative," she added absently. " That's a purely Indian vegetable, Mr. Pond. Rather sticky, and without the ghost of a flavour; but you ought to try it, as an experience, don't you think?"

It occurred to Mrs. Daye sometimes that Mr. Ancram was unreasonably difficult to entertain, even for a Chief Secretary. It occurred to her more forcibly than usual on this particular evening, and it was almost with trepidation that she produced the trump card on which she had been relying to provoke a lively suit of amiabilities. She produced it awkwardly too; there was always a slight awkwardness, irritating to so *habile* a lady, in her manner of addressing Mr. Ancram, owing to her confessed and painful inability to call him "Lewis"—yet. "Oh," she said finally, "I haven't congratulated you on your 'Modern Influence of the Vedic Books.' I assure you, in spite of its being in blue paper covers and printed by Government I went through it with the greatest interest. And there were no pictures either," Mrs. Daye added, with the ingenuousness which often clings to Anglo-Indian ladies somewhat late in life.

Mr. Ancram was occupied for the moment in scrutinising the contents of a dish which a servant patiently presented to his left elbow. It was an ornate and mottled conception visible through a mass of brown jelly, and the man looked disappointed when so important a guest, after perceptible deliberation, decisively removed his eyeglass and shook his head. Mrs. Daye was in the act of reminding herself of the probably impaired digestion of a Chief Secretary, when he seemed suddenly recalled to the fact that she had spoken.

"Really?" he said, looking fully at her, with a smile that had many qualities of compensation. "My dear Mrs. Daye, that was doing a good deal for friendship, wasn't it?"

His eyes were certainly blue and expressive when he allowed them to be, his hostess thought, and he had the straight, thin, well-indicated nose which she liked, and a sensitive mouth for a man. His work as part of the great intelligent managing machine of the Government of India overimpressed itself upon the stamp of scholarship Oxford had left on his face, which had the pallor of Bengal, with fatigued lines about the eyes, lines that suggested to Mr. Ancram's friends the constant reproach of over-exertion. A light moustache, sufficiently well-curled and worldly, effectually prevented any tinge of asceticism which might otherwise have been characteristic, and placed Mr. Ancram among those who discussed Meredith, had an expensive taste in handicrafts, and subscribed to the *Figaro Salon*. His secretary's stoop was not a pronounced and local curve, rather a general thrusting forward of his personality which was fitting enough in a scientific investigator; and his long, nervous, white hands spoke of a multitude of well-phrased Resolutions. It was ridiculous, Mrs. Daye thought, that with so agreeable a manner he should still convey the impression that one's interest in the Vedic Books was not of the least importance. It must be that she was over-sensitive. But she would be piqued notwithstanding. Pique, when one is plump and knows how to hold oneself, is more effective than almost any other attitude.

"You are exactly like all the rest! You

think that no woman can possibly care to read anything but novels! Now, as a matter of fact I am *devoted* to things like Vedic Books. If I had nothing else to do I should dig and delve in the archaic from morning till night."

"The implication being," returned Mr. Ancram sweetly, "that I have nothing else to do."

Mrs. Daye compressed her lips in the manner of one whose patience is at an end. "It would serve you perfectly right," she exclaimed, "if I didn't tell you what a long review of it I saw the other day in one of the home papers."

Ancram looked up with an almost imperceptible accession of interest.

"How nice!" he said lightly. "A fellow out here always feels himself in luck when his odds and ends get taken up at home. You don't happen to remember the paper—or the date?"

"I'm almost sure it was the *Times*," Mrs. Daye replied, with rather an accentuation of rejoiceful zeal; "but Richard can tell you. It was he who drew my attention to the notice."

Mr. Ancram's eyebrows underwent a slight contraction. "Notice" did not seem to be a felicitous word.

"Oh, thanks," he said. "Never mind; one generally comes across those things sooner or later."

"I say, Ancram," put in Mr. St. George, who had been listening on Mrs. Daye's left, "you Asiatic Society fellows won't get as much out of Church for your investigations as you did out of Spence."

Ancram looked fixedly at a porcelain cherub that moored a boatful of pink-and-white confectionery to the nearest bank of the Viceregal roses. "Sir Griffiths was certainly generous," he said. "He gave Pierson a quarter of a lakh, for instance, to get his ethnological statistics together. It was easy to persuade him to recognise the value of these things."

"It won't be easy to get this man to recognise it," persisted St. George. "He's the sort of fellow who likes sanitation better than Sanscrit. He's got a great scheme on for improving the village water-supply for Bengal, and I hear he wants to reorganise the vaccination business. Great man for the people!"

"Wants to spend every blessed pice on the bloomin' ryot," remarked Captain Delaine, with humorous resentment.

"Let us hope the people will be grateful," said Ancram vaguely.

"They won't, you know," remarked Rhoda Daye to Mr. Pond. "They'll never know. They are like the cattle—they plough and eat and sleep; and if a tenth of them die of cholera from bad water, they say it was written upon their foreheads; and if Government cleans the tanks and the tenth are spared, they say it is a good year and the gods are favourable."

"Dear me!" said Mr. Pond: "that's very interesting."

"Isn't it? And there's lots more of it—all in the Calcutta newspapers, Mr. Pond: you should read them if you wish to be informed." And Mr. Pond thought that an excellent idea.

When a Lieutenant-Governor drops into the conversational vortex of a Calcutta dinner-party he circles on indefinitely. The measure of his hospitality, the nature of his tastes, the direction of his policy, his quality as a master, and the measure of his popularity, are only a few of the heads under which he is discussed; while his wife is made the most of separately, with equal thoroughness and precision. Just before Mrs. Daye looked smilingly at Mrs. St. George, and the ladies flocked away, some one asked who Mrs. Church's friends were in Calcutta, anyway: she seemed to know hardly any one person more than another—a delightful impartiality, the lady added, of course, after Lady Spence's favouritism. The remark fell lightly enough upon the air, but Lewis Ancram did not let it pass. He looked at nobody in particular, but into space: it was a way he had when he let fall anything definite.

"Well," he said, "I hope I may claim to be one. My pretension dates back five years—I used to know them in Kaligurh. I fancy Mrs. Church will be appreciated in Calcutta. She is that combination which is so much less rare than it used to be—a woman who is as fine as she is clever, and as clever as she is charming."

"With all due deference to Mr. Ancram's opinion," remarked Mrs. Daye publicly, with one hand upon the banister, as the ladies went up to the drawing-room, "I should *not* call Mrs. Church a fine woman. She's much too slender— really almost thin!"

"My dear mummie," exclaimed Rhoda, as Mrs. St. George expressed her entire concurrence," don't be stupid! He didn't mean that."

Later Ancram stepped out of one of the open French windows and found her alone on the broad verandah, where orchids hung from the roof and big plants in pots made a spiky gloom in the corners. A tank in the garden glistened motionless below; the heavy fronds of a clump of sago palms waved up and down uncertainly in the moonlight. Now and then in the moist, soft air the scent of some hidden temple tree made itself felt. A cluster of huts to the right in the street they looked down upon stood half-concealed in a hanging blue cloud of smoke and fog. Far away in the suburbs the wailing cry of the jackals rose and fell and recommenced; nearer the drub-drubbing of a tom-tom announced that somewhere in the bazar they kept a marriage festival. But for themselves and the moonlight and the shadow of the creeper round the pillars, the verandah was quite empty, and through the windows came a song of Mrs. Delaine's about love's little hour. The situation made its voiceless demand, and neither of them were unconscious of it. Nevertheless he, lighting a cigarette, asked her if she would not come in and hear the music; and she said no—she liked it better there; whereat they both kept the silence that was necessary for the appreciation of Mrs. Delaine's song. When it was over, Rhoda's terrier, Buzz, came out with inquiring cordiality, and they talked of the growth of his accomplishments since Ancram had given him to her; and then, as if it were a development of the subject, Rhoda said:

"Mrs. Church has a very interesting face, don't you think?"

"Very," Ancram replied unhesitatingly.

"She looks as if she cared for beautiful things. Not only pictures and things, but beautiful conceptions—ideas, characteristics."

"I understand," Ancram returned: "she does."

There was a pause, while they listened to the wail of the jackals, which had grown wild and high and tumultuous. As it died away, Rhoda looked up with a little smile.

"I like that," she said; "it is about the only thing out here that is quite irrepressible. And —you knew her well at Kaligurh?"

"I think I may say I did," Ancram replied, tossing the end of his cigarette down among the hibiscus bushes. "My dear girl, you must come in. There is nothing like a seductive moonlight night in India to give one fever."

"I congratulate you," said Miss Daye—and her tone had a defiance which she did not intend, though one could not say that she was unaware of its cynicism—"I congratulate you upon knowing her well. It is always an advantage to know the wife of the Lieutenant-Governor well. The most delightful things come of it—Commissionerships, and all sorts of things. I hope you will make her understand the importance of the Vedic Books in their bearing upon the modern problems of government."

"You are always asking me to make acknowledgments—you want almost too many; but since it amuses you, I don't mind." Rhoda noted the little gleam in his eyes that contradicted this. "Sanscrit is to me now exactly what Greek was at Oxford—a stepping-stone, and nothing more. One must do something to distinguish oneself from the herd; and in India, thank fortune, it's easy enough. There's an enormous field, and next to nobody to beat. Bless you, a Commissariat Colonel can give himself an aureole of scientific discovery out here if he cares to try! If I hadn't taken up Sanscrit and Hinduism, I should have gone in for palæontology, or conchology, or folk-lore, or ferns. Anything does: only the less other people know about it the better; so I took Sanscrit." A combined suggestion of humour and candour gradually accumulated in Mr. Ancram's sentences, which came to a climax when he added, "You don't think it very original to discover that!"

"And the result of being distinguished from the herd?"

He shrugged his shoulders. "Well, they don't send one to administer the Andamans or Lower Burmah," he said. "They conserve one's intellectual achievements to adorn social centres of some importance, which is more agreeable. And then, if a valuable post falls vacant, one is not considered disqualified for it by being a little wiser than other people. Come now—there's a very big confession for you! But you mustn't tell. We scientists must take ourselves with awful seriousness if we want to be impressive. That's the part that bores one."

Mr. Ancram smiled down at his betrothed with distinct good-humour. He was under the impression that he had spontaneously given his soul an airing—an impression he was fond of. She listened, amused that she could evoke so much, and returned to the thing he had evaded.

"Between the Vedic Books and Mrs. Church," she said, "our future seems assured."

Ancram's soul retired again, and shut the door with a click.

"That is quite a false note," he said coolly: "Mrs. Church will have nothing to do with it."

CHAPTER III.

It became evident very soon after Miss Rhoda Daye's appearance in Calcutta that she was not precisely like the other young ladies in sailor hats and cambric blouses who arrived at the same time. For one superficial thing, anybody could see that she had less colour; and this her mother mourned openly—a girl depended so entirely for the first season on her colour. As other differences became obvious Mrs. Daye had other regrets, one of them being that Rhoda had been permitted so absolutely to fashion her own education. Mrs. Daye had not foreseen one trivial result of this, which was that her daughter, believing herself devoid of any special talent, refused to ornament herself with any special accomplishment. This, in Mrs. Daye's opinion, was carrying self-depreciation and reverence for achievement and all that sort of thing a great deal too far: a girl had no right to expect her parents to present her to the world in a state of artistic nudity. It was not in the nature of compensation that she understood the situation with the Amir and the ambitions of the National Congress; such things were almost unmentionable in Calcutta society. And it was certainly in the nature of aggravation that she showed, after the first month of it, an inexplicable indifference to every social opportunity but that of looking on. Miss Daye had an undoubted talent for looking on; and she would often exercise it—mutely, motionlessly, half hidden behind a pillar at a ball, or abandoned in a corner after dinner—until her mother was mortified enough to take her home. Presently it appeared that she had looked on sufficiently to know her ground. She made her valuation of society; she picked out the half-dozen Anglo-Indian types; it may be presumed that she classified her parents. She still looked on, but with less concentration: she began to talk. She developed a liking for the society of elderly gentlemen of eminence, and an abhorrence for that of their wives, which was considered of doubtful propriety, until the Head of the Foreign Office once congratulated himself openly upon sitting next her at dinner. After which she was regarded with indulgence, it was said in corners that she must be clever, subalterns avoided her, and her mother, taking her cue unerringly, figuratively threw up her hands and asked Heaven why she of all people should be given a *fin-de-siècle* daughter.

Privately Mrs. Daye tried to make herself believe, in the manner of the Parisian playwright, that a *succès d'estime* was infinitely to be preferred to the plaudits of the mob. I need hardly say that she was wholly successful in doing so, when Mr. Lewis Ancram contributed to the balance in favour of this opinion. Mr. Ancram was observing too: he observed in this case from shorter and shorter distances, and finally allowed himself to be charmed by what he saw. Perhaps that is not putting it quite strongly enough. He really encouraged himself to be thus charmed. He was of those who find in the automatic monotony of the Indian social machine, with its unvarying individual—a machine, he was fond of saying, the wheels of which are kept oiled with the essence of British Philistinism—a burden and a complaint. In London he would have lived with one foot in Mayfair and the other in the Strand; and there had been times when he talked of the necessity of chaining his ambition before his eyes to prevent his making the choice of a career over again, though it must be said that this violent proceeding was carried out rather as a solace to his defrauded capacity for culture than in view of any real danger. He had been accustomed to take the annually fresh young ladies in straw hats and cambric blouses who appeared in the cold weather much as he took the inevitable functions at Government House—to be politely avoided, if possible; if not, to be submitted to with the grace which might be expected from a person holding his office and drawing his emoluments. When he found that Rhoda Daye was likely to break up the surface of his blank indifference to evening parties he fostered the probability. Among all the young ladies in sailor hats and cambric blouses he saw his single chance for experience, interest, sensation; and he availed himself of it with an accumulated energy which Miss Daye found stimulating enough to induce her to exert herself, to a certain extent, reciprocally. She was not interested in the Hon. Mr. Lewis Ancram because of his reputation: other men had reputations—reputations almost as big as their paybills—who did not excite her imagination in the smallest degree. It would be easy to multiply accounts upon which Mr. Ancram did not interest Miss Daye, but it is not clear that any result would be arrived at that way, and the fact remains that she was interested. From this quiet point—she was entirely aware of its advantage—she contemplated Mr. Ancram's gradual advance along the lines of attraction with a feeling very like satisfaction. She had only to contemplate it. Ancram contributed his own impetus, and reached the point where he believed his affections involved with an artistic shock which he had anticipated for weeks as quite divinely enjoyable. She behaved amusingly when they were engaged: she made a little comedy of it, would be coaxed to no confessions and only one vow—that, as they were to go through life together, she would try always to be agreeable. If she had private questionings and secret alarms, she hid them with intrepidity; and if it seemed to her to be anything ridiculous that the wayward god should present himself behind the careful countenance and the well-starched shirt-front of early middle-age, holding an eyeglass in attenuated fingers, and mutely implying that he had been bored for years, she did not betray her impression. The thrall of their engagement made no change in her; she continued to be the same demure, slender creature, who said unexpected things, that she had been before. That he had covetable new privileges did not seem to make much difference; her chief value was still that of a clever acquaintance. She would grow more expensive in time, he thought vaguely; but several months had passed, as we have seen, without this result. On the other hand, there had been occasions when he fancied that she deliberately disassociated herself from him in that favourite pursuit of observation, in order to obtain a point of view which should command certain intellectual privacies of his. He wondered whether she would take this liberty with greater freedom when they were one and indivisible; and, while he felt it absurd to object, he wished she would be a little more communicative about what she saw.

They were to be married in March, when Ancram would take a year's furlough, and she would help him to lave his stiffened powers of artistic enjoyment in the beauties of the Parthenon and the inspirations of the Viennese galleries and the charms of Como and Maggiore. They talked a great deal of the satisfaction they expected to realise in this way. They went over it in detail, realising again and again that it must represent to him compensation for years of aridity and to her a store against the future likely to be drawn upon largely. Besides, it was a topic upon which they were quite sure of finding mutual understanding, even mutual congratulation—an excellent topic.

Meanwhile Ancram lived with Philip Doyle

in Hungerford Street under the ordinary circumstances which govern Calcutta bachelors. Doyle was a barrister. He stood, in Calcutta, upon his ability and his individuality, and as these had been observed to place him in familiar relations with Heads of Departments, it may be gathered that they gave him a sufficient elevation. People called him a "strong" man because he refused their invitations to dinner, but the statement might have had a more intelligent basis and been equally true. It would have surprised him immensely if he could have weighed the value of his own opinions, or observed the trouble which men who appropriated them took to give them a tinge of originality. He was a survival of an older school, certainly—people were right in saying that. He had preserved a courtliness of manner and a sincerity of behaviour which suggested an Anglo-India that is mostly lying under pillars and pyramids in rank Calcutta cemeteries now. He was hospitable and select—so much of both that he often experienced ridiculous annoyance at having asked men to dinner who were essentially unpalatable to him. His sensitiveness to qualities in personal contact was so great as to be a conspicuous indication, to the discerning eye, of Lewis Ancram's unbounded tact.

Circumstances had thrown the men under one roof, and even if the younger of them had not made himself so thoroughly agreeable, it would have been difficult to alter the arrangement.

It could never be said of Lewis Ancram that he did not choose his friends with taste, and in this case his discrimination had a foundation of respect which he was in the habit of freely mentioning. His admiration of Doyle was generous and frank, so generous and frank that one might have suspected a virtue in the expression of it. Notwithstanding this implication, it was entirely sincere, though he would occasionally qualify it.

"I often tell Doyle," he said once to Rhoda, "that his independence is purely a matter of circumstance. If he had the official yoke upon his neck he would kow-tow like the rest of us."

"I don't believe that," she answered quickly.

"Ah well, now that I think of it I don't particularly believe it myself. Doyle's the salt of the earth anyhow. He makes it just possible for officials like myself to swallow officialdom."

"Did it ever occur to you," she asked slowly, "to wonder what he thinks of you?"

"Oh, I daresay he likes me well enough. Irishmen never go in for analysing their friends. At all events we live together, and there are no rows."

They were driving, and the dogcart flew past the ships along the Strand—Ancram liked a fast horse—for a few minutes in silence. Then she had another question.

"Have you succeeded in persuading Mr. Doyle to—what do the newspapers say?—support you at the altar, yet?"

"No, confound him. He says it would be preposterous at his age—he's not a year older than I am! I wonder if he expects me to ask Baby Bramble, or one of those little boys in the Buffs! Anyway it won't be Doyle, for he goes to England, end of February—to get out of it, I believe."

"I'm not sorry," Rhoda answered; but it would have been difficult for her to explain, at the moment, why she was not sorry.

CHAPTER IV.

"I DON'T mind telling you," said Philip Doyle, knocking the ashes out of his pipe, "that, personally, His Acting Honour represents to me a number of objectionable things. He is a Radical, and a Low Churchman, and a Particularist. He's that objectionable ethical mixture, a compound of petty virtues. He believes this earth was created to give him an atmosphere to do his duty in; and he does it with the invincible courage of short-sightedness combined with the notion that the ultimate court of appeal for eighty million Bengalis should be his precious Methodist conscience. But the brute's honest, and if he insists on putting this University foolishness of his through, I'm sorry for him. He's a dead man, politically, the day it is announced."

"He is," replied Ancram, concentrating his

attention on a match and the end of his cigar. " There's—no doubt—about that."

The two men were smoking after dinner, with the table and a couple of decanters between them. Roses drooped over the bowl of Cutch silver that gleamed in the middle of the empty cloth, and a lemon leaf or two floated in the finger-glass at Ancram's elbow. He threw the match into it, and looked across at Doyle with his cigar between his teeth in the manner which invites further discussion.

" In point of political morality I suppose he's right enough——"

" He generally is," Ancram interrupted. " He's got a scent for political morality keen enough to upset every form of Government known to the nineteenth century."

" But they see political morality through another pair of spectacles in England. To withdraw State aid from education anywhere at this end of the century is as impracticable as it would be to deprive the British workman of his vote. It's retrogressive, and this is an age which will admit anything except a mistake of its own."

"He doesn't intend to withdraw State aid from education. He means to spend the money on technical schools."

"A benevolent intention. But it won't make the case any better with the Secretary of State. He will say that it ought to be done without damaging the sacred cause of higher culture."

"Damn the sacred cause of higher culture!" replied Ancram, with an unruffled countenance. "What has it done out here? Filled every sweeper's son of them with an ambition to sit on an office stool and be a gentleman!—created by thousands a starveling class that find nothing to do but swell mass-meetings on the Maidan and talk sedition that gets telegraphed from Peshawur to Cape Comorin. I advertised for a baboo the other day, and had four hundred applications—fifteen rupees a month, poor devils! But the Dayes were a fortnight in getting a decent cook on twenty."

"Bentinck should have thought of that; it's too late now. You can't bestow a boon on the masses in a spirit of progressiveness and take it away sixty years later in a spirit of prudence. It's decent enough of Church to be willing to bear the consequences of somebody else's blunder; but blunders of that kind have got to take their place in the world's formation and let the ages retrieve them. It's the only way."

"Oh, I agree with you. Church is an ass: he ought not to attempt it."

"Why do you fellows let him?"

Ancram looked in Doyle's direction as he answered—looked near him, fixed his eyes, with an effect of taking a view at the subject round a corner, upon the other man's tobacco-jar. The trick annoyed Doyle; he often wished it were the sort of thing one could speak about.

"Nobody is less amenable to reason," he said, "than the man who wants to hit his head against a stone wall, especially if he thinks the world will benefit by his inconvenience. And, to make matters worse, Church has complicated the thing with an idea of his duty toward the people at home who send out the missionaries. He doesn't think it exactly according to modern ethics that they should take up collections in village churches to provide the salvation of the higher mathematics for the sons of fat *bunnias* in the bazar—who could very well afford to pay for it themselves."

" He can't help that."

Ancram finished his claret. " I believe he has some notion of advertising it. And after he has eliminated the missionary who teaches the Georgics instead of the Gospels, and devoted the educational grants to turning the gentle Hindoo into a skilled artisan, he thinks the cause of higher culture may be pretty much left to take care of itself. He believes we could bleed Linsettiah and Pattore and some of those chaps for endowments, I fancy, though he doesn't say so."

" Better try some of the smaller natives. A maharajah won't do much for a C. I. E. or an extra gun nowadays: it isn't good enough. He knows that all Europe is ready to pay him the honours of royalty whenever he chooses to tie up his cooking-pots and go there. He'll save his money and buy hand-organs with it, or panoramas, or sewing-machines. Presently, if this adoration of the Eastern potentate goes on at home, we shall have the maharajah whom we propose to honour receiving our proposition with his thumb applied to his nose and all his fingers out!"

Ancram yawned. "Well, it won't be a question of negotiating for endowments: it will never come off. Church will only smash himself over the thing if he insists; and," he added, as one who makes an unprejudiced, impartial statement on fatalistic grounds, "he will insist. I should find the whole business rather amusing if, as Secretary, I hadn't to be the mouthpiece for it." He looked at his watch. "Half-past nine. I suppose I ought to be off. You're not coming?"

"Where?"

"To Belvedere. A 'walk-round,' I believe."

"Thanks: I think not. It would be too much bliss for a corpulent gentleman of my years. I remember—the card came last week, and I gave it to Mohammed to take care of. I believe Mohammed keeps a special *almirah* for the purpose; and in it," Mr. Doyle continued gravely, "are the accumulations of several seasons. He regards them as a trust only second to that of the Director of Records, and last year he made them the basis of an application for more pay."

"Which you gave him," laughed Ancram, getting into his light overcoat as the brougham rolled up to the door. "I loathe going; but for me there's no alternative. There seems to be an Act somewhere providing that a man in my peculiar position must show himself in society."

"So long as you hover on the brink of matrimony," said the other, "you must be a butterfly. Console yourself: after you take the plunge you can turn ascidian if you like."

The twinkle went out of Philip Doyle's eyes as he heard the carriage door shut and the wheels roll crunching toward the gate. He filled his pipe again and took up the *Saturday Review*. Half an hour later he was looking steadily at the wall over the top of that journal, considering neither its leading articles nor its reviews nor its advertisements, but Mr. Lewis Ancram's peculiar position.

At that moment Ancram leaned against the wall in a doorway of the drawing-room at Belvedere, one leg lightly crossed over the other, his right hand in his pocket, dangling his eyeglass with his left. It was one of the many casual attitudes in which the world was informed that a Chief Secretary, in Mr. Ancram's opinion, had no prescriptive right to give himself airs. He had a considering look: one might have said that his mind was far from the occasion—perhaps upon the advisability of a tobacco tax; but this would not have been correct. He was really thinking of the quantity and the quality of the people who passed him, and whether as a function the thing could be considered a success. With the white gleam on the pillars, and the palms everywhere, and the moving vista of well-dressed women through long, richly-furnished rooms arranged for a large reception, it was certainly pretty enough; but there was still the question of individuals, which had to be determined by such inspection as he was bestowing upon them. It would have been evident to anybody that more people recognised Ancram than

Ancram recognised; he had by no means the air of being on the look-out for acquaintances. But occasionally some such person as the Head of the Telegraph Department looked well at him and said, "How do, Ancram?" with the effect of adding "I defy you to forget who I am!" or a lady of manner gave him a gracious and pronounced inclination, which also said, "You are the clever, the rising Mr. Ancram. You haven't called; but you are known to despise society. I forgive you, and I bow." One or two Members of Council merely vouchsafed him a nod as they passed; but it was noticeably only Members of Council who nodded to Mr. Ancram. An aide-de-camp to the Viceroy, however—a blue-eyed younger son with his mind seriously upon his duty—saw Ancram in his path, and hesitated. He had never quite decided to what extent these fellows in the Bengal Secretariat, and this one in particular, should be recognised by an aide-de-camp; and he went round the other way. Presently there was a little silken stir and rustle, a parting of the ladies' trains, and a lull of observation along both sides of the lane which suddenly formed itself among the people. His Excellency the Viceroy had taken his early leave and was making his departure. Lord Scansleigh had an undisguised appreciation of an able man, and there was some definiteness in the way he stopped, though it was but for a moment, and shook hands with Ancram, who swung the eyeglass afterwards more casually than he had done before. The aide-de-camp, following after, was in no wise rebuked. What the Viceroy chose to do threw no light on his difficulty. He merely cast his eyes upon the floor, and his fresh coloured countenance expressed a respectfully sad admiration for the noble manner in which his lord discharged every obligation pertaining to the Viceregal office.

The most privileged hardly cares to make demands upon his hostess as long as she has a Viceroy to entertain, and Ancram waited until their Excellencies were well on their way home, their four turbaned Sikhs trotting after them, before he made any serious attempt to find Mrs. Church. A sudden and general easefulness was observable at the same time. People began to look about them and walk and talk with the consciousness that it was no longer possible that they should be suspected of arranging themselves so that Lord Scansleigh *must* bow. The Viceroy having departed, they thought about other things. She was standing, when presently he made his way to her, talking to Sir William Scott of the Foreign Department, and at the moment, to the Maharajah of Pattore. Ancram paused and watched her unperceived. It was like the pleasure of looking at a picture one technically understands. He noted with satisfaction the subtle difference in her manner toward the two men, and how, in her confidence with the one and her condescending recognition of the other's dignity, both were consciously receiving their due. He noticed the colour of her heliotrope velvet gown, and asked himself whether any other woman in the room could possibly wear that shade. Mentally he dared the other women to say that its simplicity was over-dramatic, or that by the charming arrangement of her hair and her pearls and the yellowed lace, that fell over her shoulders Judith Church had made herself too literal a representation of a great-grandmother who certainly wore none of these things. He paused another second to catch the curve of her white throat as she turned her head with a little characteristic lifting of her chin; and then he went up to her. The definite purpose that appeared in his face was enough of itself to assert their intimacy—to this end it was not necessary that he should drop his eyeglass.

"Oh," she said, with a step forward, "how do you do! I began to think——Maharajah, when you are invited to parties you always come, don't you? Well, this gentleman does not always come, I understand. I beg you will ask a question about it at the next meeting of the Legislative Council. The Honourable the Chief Secretary is requested to furnish an explanation of his lamentable failure to perform his duties toward society."

The native smiled uncomfortably, puzzled at her audacity. His membership of the Bengal Legislative Council was a new toy, and he was not sure that he liked any one else to play with it.

"His Highness of Pattore," said Ancram, slipping a hand under the fat elbow in its pink-and-gold brocade, "would be the very last fellow to get me into a scrape. Wouldn't you, Maharaj!"

His Highness beamed affectionately upon Ancram. There was, at all events, nothing but flattery in being taken by the elbow by a Chief Secretary. "Certainlie," he replied—"the verrie last"; and he laughed the unctuous, irresponsible laugh of a maharajah, which is accompanied by the twinkling of pendant emeralds and the shaking of personal rotundities which cannot be indicated.

Sir William Scott folded his arms and refolded them, balanced himself once or twice on the soles of his shoes, pushed out his under-lip, and retreated in the gradual and surprised way which would naturally be adopted by the Foreign Department when it felt itself left out of the conversation. The Maharajah stood about uneasily on one leg for a moment, and then with a hasty double salaam he too waddled away. Mrs. Church glanced after his retreating figure—

it was almost a perfect oval—with lips prettily composed to seemly gravity. Then, as her eyes met Ancram's, she laughed like a schoolgirl.

"Oh," she said, "go away! I mustn't talk to you. I shall be forgetting my part."

"You are doing it well. Lady Spence, at this stage of the proceedings, was always surrounded by bank-clerks and policemen. I do not observe a member of either of those interesting species," he said, glancing round through his eyeglass, "within twenty yards. On the contrary, an expectant Member of Council on the nearest sofa, the Commander-in-Chief hovering in the middle distance, and a fringe of Departmental Heads on the horizon."

"I do not see any of them," she laughed, looking directly at Ancram. "We are going to sit down, you and I, and talk for four or six minutes, as the last baboo said who implored an interview with my husband"; and Mrs. Church sank, with just a perceptible turning of her shoulder upon the world, into the nearest armchair. It was a wide gilded arm-chair, cushioned in deep yellow silk. Ancram thought, as she crossed her feet and leaned her head against the back of it, that the effect was delicious.

"And you really think I am doing it well!" she said. "I have been dying to know. I really dallied for a time with the idea of asking one of the aides-de-camp. But as a matter of fact," she said confidentially, "though I order them about most callously, I am still horribly afraid of the aides-de-camp—in uniform, on duty."

"And in flannels, off duty?"

"In flannels, off duty, I make them almond toffee and they tell me their love affairs. I am their sisterly mother and their cousinly aunt. We even have games of ball."

"They are nice boys," he said, with a sigh of resignation: "I daresay they deserve it."

There was an instant's silence of good fellowship, and then she moved her foot a little, so that a breadth of the heliotrope velvet took on a paler light.

"Yes," he nodded, "it is quite—regal."

She laughed, flushing a little. "Really! That's not altogether correct. It ought to be only officiating. But I can't tell you how delicious it is to be *obliged* to wear pretty gowns."

At that moment an Additional Member of Council passed them so threateningly that Mrs. Church was compelled to put out a staying hand and inquire for Lady Bloomsbury, who was in England, and satisfy herself that Sir Peter had quite recovered from his bronchitis, and warn Sir Peter against Calcutta's cold-weather fogs. Ancram kept his seat, but Sir Peter stood with stout persistence, rooted in his rights. It was only when Mrs. Church asked him whether he had seen the new portrait, and told him where it was, that he moved on, and then he believed that he went of his own accord. By the time an Indian official arrives at an Additional Membership he is usually incapable of perceiving anything which does not tend to enhance that dignity.

"You have given two of my six minutes to somebody else, remember," Ancram said. For an instant she did not answer him. She was looking about her with a perceptible air of having, for the moment, been oblivious of something it was her business to remember. Almost immediately her eye discovered John Church. He was in conversation with the Bishop, and apparently they were listening to each other with deference, but sometimes Church's gaze wandered vaguely over the heads of the people and sometimes he looked at the floor. His hands were clasped in front of him, his chin was so sunk in his chest that the most conspicuous part of him seemed his polished forehead and his heavy black eyebrows, his expression was that of a man who submits to the inevitable. Ancram saw him at the same moment, and in the silence that asserted itself between them there was a touch of embarrassment which the man found sweet. He felt a foolish impulse to devote himself to turning John Church into an ornament to society.

"This sort of thing——" he suggested condoningly.

"Bores him. Intolerably. He grudges the time and the energy. He says there is so much to do."

"He is quite right."

"Oh, don't encourage him! On the contrary—promise me something."

"Anything."

"When you see him standing about alone—he is really very absent-minded—go up and make him talk to you. He will get your ideas—the time, you see, will not be wasted. And neither will the general public," she added, "be confronted with the spectacle of a Lieutenant-Governor who looks as if he had a contempt for his own hospitality."

"I'll try. But I hardly think my ideas upon points of administration are calculated to enliven a social evening. And don't send me now. The Bishop is doing very well."

"The Bishop?" She turned to him again, with laughter in the dark depths of her eyes. "I realised the other day what one may attain to in Calcutta. His Lordship asked me, with some timidity, what I thought of the length of his sermons! Tell me, please, who is this madam bearing down upon me in pink and grey?"

Ancram was on his feet. "It is Mrs. Daye,"

he said. "People who come so late ought not to insist upon seeing you."

"Mrs. Daye! Oh, of course; your——" But Mrs. Daye was clasping her hostess's hand. "And Miss Daye, I think," said Mrs. Church, looking frankly into the face of the girl behind, "whom I have somehow been defrauded of meeting before. I have a great many congratulations to—divide," she went on prettily, glancing at Ancram. "Mr. Ancram is an old friend of ours."

"Thank you," replied Miss Daye. Her manner suggested that at school such acknowledgments had been very carefully taught her.

"My dear, you should make a pretty curtsey," her mother said jocularly, and then looked at Rhoda with astonishment as the girl, with an unmoved countenance, made it.

Ancram looked uncomfortable, but Mrs. Church cried out with vivacity that it was charming—she was so glad to find that Miss Daye could unbend to a stranger; and Mrs. Daye immediately stated that she *must* hear whether the good news was true that Mrs.

Church had accepted the presidency—presidentship (what should one say?)—of the Lady Dufferin Society. Ah! that was delightful—now *everything* would go smoothly. Poor dear Lady Spence found it *far* too much for her! Mrs. Daye touched upon a variety of other matters as the four stood together, and the gaslights shone down upon the diamond stars in the women's hair, and the band played on the verandah behind the palms. Among them was the difficulty of getting seats in the Cathedral in the cold weather, and the fascinating prospect of having a German man-of-war in port for the season, and that dreadful frontier expedition against the Nagapis; and they ran, in the end, into an allusion to Mrs. Church's delightful Thursday tennises.

"Ah, yes," Mrs. Church replied, as the lady gave utterance to this, with her dimpled chin thrust over her shoulder, in the act of departure: "you must not forget my Thursdays. And you," she said to Rhoda, with a directness which she often made very engaging—"you will come too, I hope?"

"Oh, yes, thank you," the girl answered, with her neat smile: "I will come too—with pleasure."

"Why didn't you go with them?" Mrs. Church exclaimed a moment later.

Ancram looked meditatively at the chandelier. "We are not exactly a demonstrative couple," he said. "She likes a decent reticence, I believe—in public. I'll find them presently."

They were half a mile on their way home when he began to look for them; and Mrs. Daye had so far forgotten herself as to comment unfavourably upon his behaviour.

"My dear mummie," her daughter responded, "you don't suppose I want to interfere with his amusements!"

CHAPTER V.

A BAZAR had been opened in aid of a Cause. The philanthropic heart of Calcutta, laid bare, discloses many Causes, and during the cold weather their commercial hold upon the community is as briskly maintained as it may be consistently with the modern doctrine of the liberty of the subject. The purpose of this bazar was to bring the advantages of the piano and feather-stitch and Marie Bashkirtseff to young native ladies of rank. It had been for some time obvious that young native ladies of rank were painfully behind the van of modern progress. It was known that they were not in the habit of spending the golden Oriental hours in the search for wisdom as the bee obtains honey from the flowers: they much preferred sucking their own fingers, cloyed with sweetmeats from the bazar. Yet a few of them had tasted emancipation. Their husbands allowed them to show their faces to the world. Of one, who had been educated in London, it was whispered that she wore stays, and read books in three languages besides Sanscrit, and ate of the pig! These the memsahibs fastened upon and infected with the idea of elevating their sisters by annual appeals to the public based on fancy articles. Future generations of Aryan lady-voters, hardly as yet visible in the effulgence of all that is to come, will probably fail to understand that their privileges were founded, towards the end of the nineteenth century, on an antimacassar; but thus it will have been.

The wife of the Lieutenant-Governor had opened the bazar. She had done it in black lace and jet, which became her exceedingly, with a pretty little speech, which took due account of the piano and feather-stitch and Marie Bashkirtseff under more impressive names. She had driven there with Lady Scott. The way was very long and very dusty and very native, which includes several other undesirable characteristics; and Lady Scott had beguiled it with details of an operation she had insisted on witnessing at the Dufferin Hospital for Women. Lady Scott declared that, holding the position she did on the Board, she really felt the responsibility of seeing that things were properly done, but that henceforth the lady-doctor in charge should have her entire confidence. "I only wonder," said Mrs. Church, "that, holding the position you do on the Board, you didn't insist on performing the operation yourself"; and her face was so grave that Lady Scott felt flattered and deprecated the idea.

Then they had arrived and walked with circumstance through the little desultory crowd of street natives up the strip of red cloth to the door, and there been welcomed by three or four of the very most emancipated, with two beautiful, flat, perfumed bouquets of pink-and-white roses and many suffused smiles. And then the little speech, which gave Mrs. Gasper of the High Court the most poignant grief, in that men, on account of the unemancipated, were excluded from the occasion; she would simply have given anything to have had her husband hear it. After which Mrs. Church had gone from counter to counter, with her duty before her eyes. She bought daintily, choosing Dacca muslins and false gods, brass plaques from Persia and embroidered cloths from Kashmir. A dozen or two of the unemancipated pressed softly upon her, chewing betel, and appraising the value of her investments, and little Mrs. Gasper noted them too from the other side of the room. Lady Scott was most kind in showing dear Mrs. Church desirable purchases, and made, herself, conspicuously more than the wife of the Lieutenant-Governor. On every hand a native lady said, "Buy something!" with an accent less expressive of entreaty than of resentful expectation. One of the emancipated went behind a door and made up the total of Mrs. Church's expenditure. She came out again looking discontented: Lady Spence the year before had spent half as much again.

Mrs. Church felt as she drove away that she had left behind her an injury which might properly find redress under a Regulation.

She was alone, Lady Scott having to go on to

a meeting of the "Board" with Mrs. Gasper. The disc of pink-and-white roses rolled about with the easy motion of the barouche, on the opposite seat. It was only half-past four, and the sun was still making strong lines with the tawdry flat-roofed yellow shops that huddled along the crowded interminable streets. She looked out and saw a hundred gold-bellied wasps hovering over a tray of glistening sweetmeats. Next door a woman with her red cloth pulled over her head, and her naked brown baby on her hip, paused and bought a measure of parched corn from a bunnia, who lolled among his grain heaps a fat invitation to hunger. Then came the square dark hole of Abdul Rahman, where he sat in his spectacles and sewed, with his long lean legs crossed in front of him, and half a dozen red-beaked love-birds in a wicker cage to keep him company. And then the establishment of Saddanath Mookerjee, announcing in a dazzling fringe of black letters:

```
PAINS FEVERANDISEASES CURED
       WHILE YOU WAIT
```

She looked at it all as she rolled by with a little tender smile of reconnaissance. The old fascination never failed her; the people and their doings never became common facts. Nevertheless she was very tired. The crowd seethed along in the full glare of the afternoon, hawking, disputing, gesticulating. The burden of their talk—the naked coolies, the shrill-jabbering women with loads of bricks upon their heads, the sleek baboos in those European shirts the nether hem of which no canon of propriety has ever taught them to confine—the burden of their talk reached her where she sat, and it was all of *paisa* * and *rupia*, the eternal dominant note of the bazar. She closed her eyes and tried to put herself into relation with a life bounded by the rim of a copper coin. She was certainly very tired. When she looked again a woman stooped over one of the city standpipes and made a cup with her hand and gave her little son to drink. He was a very beautiful little son, with a string of blue beads round his neck and a silver anklet

---

* Halfpence.

on each of his fat brown legs, and as he caught her hand with his baby fingers the mother smiled over him in her pride.

Judith Church suddenly leaned back among her cushions very close to tears. " It would have been better," she said to herself—" so much better," as she opened her eyes widely and tried to think about something else. There was her weekly dinner-party of forty that night, and she was to go down with the Bishop. Oh, well! that was better than Sir Peter Bloomsbury. She hoped Captain Thrush had not forgotten to ask some people who could sing—and *not* Miss Nellie Vansittart. She smiled a little as she thought how Captain Thrush had made Nellie Vansittart's pretty voice an excuse for asking her and her people twice already this month. She must see that Captain Thrush was not on duty the afternoon of Mrs. Vansittart's *musicale*. She felt indulgent towards Captain Thrush and Nellie Vansittart; she give that young lady plenary absolution for the monopoly of her lieutenant on the Belvedere Thursdays; she thought of them by their Christian names.

Then to-morrow—to-morrow she opened the *café chantant* for the Sailors' Home, and they dined at the Fort with the General. On Wednesday there was the Eurasian Female Orphans' prize-giving, and the dance on board the *Boctia*. On Friday a "Lady Dufferin" meeting—or was it the Dhurrumtollah Self-Help Society, or the Sisters' Mission?—she must look it up in her book. And, sandwiched in somewhere, she knew there was a German bacteriologist and a lecture on astronomy. She put up both her slender hands in her black gloves and yawned; remembering at the same time that it was ten days since she had seen Lewis Ancram. Her responsibilities, when he mocked at them with her, seemed light and amusing. He gave her strength and stimulus: she was very frank with herself in confessing how much she depended upon him.

The carriage drew up on one side of the stately width of Chowringhee. That is putting it foolishly; for Chowringhee has only one side to draw up at—the other is a footpath bordering the great green Maidan, which stretches on across to the river's edge, and is fringed with masts from Portsmouth and Halifax and Ispahan. When the sun goes down behind them—— But the sun had not gone down when Mrs. Church got out of her carriage and went up the steps of the School of Art: it was still burnishing the red bricks of that somewhat insignificant building, and lying in yellow sheets over the vast stucco bulk of the Indian Museum on one side, and playing among the tree-tops in the garden of the Commissioner of Police on the other. Anglo-Indian aspirations, in their wholly subordinate, artistic form, were gathered together in an exhibition here, and here John Church, who was inspecting a gaol at the other end of Calcutta, had promised to meet his wife at five o'clock.

The Lieutenant-Governor had been looking forward to this: it was so seldom, he said, that he found an opportunity of combining a duty and a pleasure. Judith Church remembered other Art Exhibitions she had seen in India, and thought that one category was enough.

At the farther end of the room a native gentleman stood transfixed with admiration before a portrait of himself by his own son. Two or three ladies with catalogues darted hurriedly, like humming-birds, from water-colour to water-colour. A cadaverous planter from the Terai, who turned out sixty thousand pounds of good tea and six yards of bad pictures annually, talked with conviction to an assenting broker with his thumbs in the armholes of his waistcoat, about the points of his "Sunset View of Kinchinjunga," that hung among the oils on the other wall. There was no one else in the room but Mr. Lewis Ancram, who wore a straw hat and an air of non-expectancy, and looked a sophisticated twenty-five.

For a moment, although John Church was the soul of punctuality, it did not seem remarkable to Mrs. Church that her husband had failed to turn up. Ancram had begun to explain, indeed, before it occurred to her to ask; and this, when she remembered it, brought a delicate flush to her cheeks which stayed there, and suggested to the Chief Secretary the pleasant recollection of a certain dewy little translucent flower that grew among the Himalayan mosses very high up.

"It was a matter His Honour thought really required looking into—clear evidence, you know, that the cholera was actually being communicated inside the gaol—and when I offered to bring his apologies on to you I honestly believe he was delighted to secure another hour of investigation."

"John works atrociously hard," she replied; and when he weighed this afterward, as he had begun to weigh the things she said, he found in it appreciably more concern for John's regrettable habit of working atrociously hard than vexation at his failure to keep their engagement.

They walked about for five minutes and looked at the aspirations. Ancram remembered Rhoda Daye's hard little sayings on the opening day, and reflected that some women could laugh with a difference. Mrs. Church did it with greatest freedom, he noticed, at the prize pictures. For the others she had compunction, and she regarded the "Sunset View of Kinchinjunga" with a smile that she plainly atoned for by an inward tear. "Don't!" she said, looking round the walls, as he invested that peak with the character of a strawberry ice. "It means all the bloom of their lives, poor things. At all events it's ideality, it isn't——"

"Pig-sticking!"

"Yes," she said softly. "If I knew what in the world to do with it, I would buy that 'Kinchin.' But its ultimate disposal does present difficulties."

"I don't think you would have any right to do that, you know. You couldn't be so dishonest with the artist. Who would sell the work of his hand to be burned!"

He was successful in provoking her appreciation. "You are quite right," she said. "The patronage of my pity! You always see!"

"I *have* bought a picture," Ancram went on, "by a fellow named Martin, who seems to have sent it out from England. It's nothing great, but I thought it was a pity to let it go back. That narrow one, nearest to the corner."

"It is good enough to escape getting a prize," she laughed. "Yes, I like it rather—a good deal

—very much indeed. I wish I were a critic and could tell you why. It will be a pleasure to you; it is so green and cool and still."

Mr. Ancram's purchase was of the type that is growing common enough at the May exhibitions—a bit of English landscape on a dull day towards evening, fields and a bank with trees on it, a pool with water-weeds in it, the sky crowding down behind and standing out in front in the quiet water. Perhaps it lacked imagination—there was no young woman leaning out of the canoe to gather water-lilies—but it had been painted with a good deal of knowledge.

Mr. James Springgrove at the moment was talking about it to another gentleman. Mr. Springgrove was one of Calcutta's humourists. He was also a member of the Board of Revenue; and for these reasons, combined with his subscription, it was originally presumed that Mr. Springgrove understood Art. People generally thought he did, because he was a Director and a member of the Hanging Committee, but this was a mistake. Mr. Springgrove brought his head as nearly as possible into a line with the

There was a moment's pause.

other gentleman's head, from which had issued, in weak commendation, the statement that No. 223 reminded it of home.

"If you asked what it reminded *me* of," said Mr. Springgrove, clapping the other on the back, "I should say verdigris, sir—verdigris."

Mrs. Church and the Honourable Mr. Lewis Ancram looked into each other's eyes and smiled as long as there was any excuse for smiling.

"I am glad you are not a critic," he said. She was verging toward the door. "What are you going to do now?"

"Afterward—we meant to drive to Hastings House. John thought there would be time. It is quite near Belvedere, you know. But—— And I shall not have another free afternoon for a fortnight."

They went out in silence, past the baboo who sat behind a table at the receipt of entrance money, and down the steps. The syce opened the carriage door, and Mrs. Church got in. There was a moment's pause, while the man looked questioningly at Ancram, still holding open the door.

"If he invites himself," said Judith inwardly, with the intention of self-discipline; and the rest was hope.

"Is there any reason——?" he asked, with his foot on the step; and it was quite unnecessary that he should add "against my coming?"

"No—there is no reason." Then she added, with a visible effort to make it the commonplace thing it was not, "Then you will drive out with me, and I shall see the place after all? How nice!"

They rolled out into the gold-and-green afternoon life of the Maidan, along wide pipal-shadowed roads, across a bridge, through a lane or two where the pariahs barked after the carriage and the people about the huts stared, shading their eyes. There seemed very little to say. They thought themselves under the spell of the pleasantness of it—the lifting of the burden and the heat of the day, the little wind that shook the fronds of the date palms and stole about bringing odours from where the people were cooking, the unyoked oxen, the hoarse home-going talk of the crows that flew city-ward against the yellow sky with a purple light on their wings.

"Let the carriage stay here," Judith said, as they stopped beside a dilapidated barred gate. "I want to walk to the house."

A salaaming creature in a *dhoty* hurried out of a clump of bamboos in the corner and flung open the gate. It seemed to close again upon the world. They were in an undulating waste that had once been a stately pleasure-ground, and it had a visible soul that lived upon its memories and was content in its abandonment. It was so still that the great teak leaves, twisted and discoloured and full of holes like battered bronze, dropping singly and slowly through the mellow air, fell at their feet with little rustling cracks.

"What a perfection of silence!" Judith exclaimed softly; and then some vague perception impelled her to talk of other things—of her dinner-party and Nellie Vansittart.

Ancram looked on, as it were, at her conversation for a moment or two with his charming smile. Then, "Oh, dear lady," he broke in, "let them go—those people. They are the vulgar considerations of the time which has been—which will be again. But this is a pause—made for *us*."

She looked down at the rusty teak-leaves, and he almost told her, as he knocked them aside, how poetic a shadow clung round her eyelids. The curve of the drive brought them to the old stucco mansion, dreaming quietly and open-eyed over its great square porch of the Calcutta of Nuncomar and Philip Francis.

"It broods, doesn't it?" said Judith Church, standing under the yellow honeysuckle of the porch. "Don't you wish you could see the ghost!"

The gatekeeper reappeared, and stood offering them each a rose.

"This gentleman," replied Ancram, "will know all about the ghost. He probably makes his living out of Warren Hastings, in the tourist season. Without doubt, he says, there is a *bhut*, a very terrible *bhut*, which lives in the room directly over our heads and wears iron boots. Shall we go and look for it?"

Half way up the stairs Ancram turned and saw the gatekeeper following them. "You have leave to go," he said in Hindustani.

At the top he turned again, and found the man still salaaming at their heels. "*Jao!*" he shouted, with a threatening movement, and the native fled.

"It is preposterous," he said apologetically to Mrs. Church, "that one should be dogged everywhere by these people."

They explored the echoing rooms, and looked down the well of the ruined staircase, and decided that no ghost with the shadow of a title to the property could let such desirable premises go unhaunted. They were in absurdly good spirits. They had not been alone together for a fortnight. The sky was all red in the west as they stepped out upon the wide flat roof, and the warm light that was left seemed to hang in mid-air. The spires and domes of Calcutta lay under a sulphur-coloured haze, and the palms on the horizon stood in filmy clouds. The beautiful tropical day was going out.

"We must go in ten minutes," said Judith, sitting down on the low mossy parapet.

"Back into the world." He reflected hastily and decided. Up to this time Rhoda Daye had been a conventionality between them. He had a sudden desire to make her the subject of a confidence—to explain, perhaps to discuss, anyhow to explain.

"Tell me, my friend," he said, making a pattern on the lichen of the roof with his stick, "what do you think of my engagement?"

She looked up startled. It was as if the question had sprung at her. She too felt the need of a temporary occupation, and fell upon her rose.

"You had my congratulations a long time ago," she said, carefully shredding each petal into three.

"Don't!" he exclaimed impatiently: "I'm serious!"

"Well, then—it is not a fair thing that you are asking me. I don't know Miss Daye. I never shall know her. To me she is a little marble image with a very pretty polish."

"And to me also," he repeated, seizing her

words: " she is a little marble image with a very pretty polish." He put an unconscious demand for commiseration into his tone. Doubtless he did not mean to go so far, but his inflection added, " And I've got to marry her!"

"To you—to you!" She plucked aimlessly at her rose, and searched vainly for something which would improve the look of his situation. But the rush of this confidence had torn up commonplaces by the roots. She felt it beating somewhere about her heart; and her concern, for the moment, in hearing of his misfortune, was for herself.

" The ironical part of it is," he went on, very pale with the effort of his candour, "that I was blindly certain of finding her sympathetic. You know what one means by that in a woman. I wanted it, just then. I seemed to have arrived at a crisis of wanting it. I made ludicrously sure of it. If you had been here," he added with conviction, " it would never have happened."

She opened her lips to say "Then I wish I had been here," but the words he heard were, " People tell me she is very clever."

"Oh," he said bitterly, "she has the qualities of her defects, no doubt. But she isn't a woman —she's an intelligence. Conceive, I beg of you, the prospect of passing one's life in conjugal relations with an intelligence!"

Judith assured herself vaguely that this brutality of language had its excuse. She could have told him very fluently that he ought not to marry Rhoda Daye under any circumstances, but something made it impossible that she should say anything of the sort. She strove with the instinct for a moment, and then, as it overthrew her, she looked about her shivering. The evening chill of December had crept in and up from the marshes; one or two street lamps twinkled out in the direction of the city; light white levels of mist had begun to spread themselves among the trees in the garden below them.

"We must go," she said, rising hurriedly: "how suddenly it has grown cold!" And as she passed before him into the empty house he saw that her face was so drawn that even he could scarcely find it beautiful.

CHAPTER VI.

"Mummie," remarked Miss Daye, as she pushed on the fingers of a new pair of gloves in the drawing-room, "the conviction grows upon me that I shall never become Mrs. Ancram."

"Rhoda, if you talk like that you will certainly bring on one of my headaches, and it will be the third in a fortnight that I'll have to thank you for. Did I or did I not send home the order for your wedding dress by last mail?"

"You did, mummie. But you could always advertise it in the local papers, you know. Could you fasten this? '*By Private Sale—A Wedding Dress originally intended for the Secretariat. Ivory Satin and Lace. Skirt thirty-nine inches, waist twenty-one. Warranted never been worn.*'. Thanks so much!"

"Rhoda! you are capable of anything——"

"Of most things, mummie, I admit. But I begin to fear, not of that!"

"Are you going to break it off? There he is this minute! Don't let him come in here, dear—he would know instantly that we had been discussing him. You *have* upset me so!"

"He shan't." Miss Daye walked to the door. "You are not to come any farther, my dear sir," said she to the Honourable Mr. Ancram among the Japanese pots on the landing: "mummie's going to have a headache, and doesn't want you. I'm quite ready!" She stood for a moment in the doorway, her pretty shoulders making admirably correct lines, in a clinging grey skirt and silver braided zouave, that showed a charming glimpse of blue silk blouse underneath, buttoning her second glove. Ancram groaned within himself that he must have proposed to her because she was *chic*. Then she looked back. "Don't worry, mummie. I'll let you know within a fortnight. You won't have to advertise it after all—you can countermand the order by telegraph!" Mrs. Daye, on the sofa, threw up her hands speechlessly, and her eyes when her daughter finally left the room were round with apprehension.

Ancram had come to take his betrothed for a drive in his dog-cart. It is a privilege Calcutta offers to people who are engaged: they are permitted to drive about together in dog-carts. The act has the binding force of a public confession. Mr. Ancram and Miss Daye had taken advantage of it in the beginning. By this time it would be more proper to say that they were taking refuge in it.

He had seen Mrs. Church several times since the evening on which he had put her into her carriage at the gates of Hastings House, and got into his own trap and driven home with a feeling which he analysed as purified but not resigned. She had been very quiet, very self-contained, apparently content to be gracious and effective in the gown of the occasion; but once or twice he fancied he saw a look of waiting, a gleam of expectancy, behind her eyes. It was this that encouraged him to ask her, at the first opportunity, whether she did not think he would be perfectly justified in bringing the thing to an end. She answered him, with an unalterable look, that she could not help him in that decision; and he brought away a sense that he had not obtained the support on which he had depended. This did not prevent him from arriving very definitely at the decision in question unaided. Nothing could be more obvious than that the girl did not care for him; and, granting this, was he morally at liberty, from the girl's own point of view, to degrade her by a marriage which was, on her side, one of pure ambition? If her affections had been involved in the remotest degree—— but he shrugged his shoulders at the idea of Rhoda Daye's affections. He wished to Heaven, like any schoolboy, that she would fall in love with somebody else, but she was too damned clever to fall in love with anybody. The thing would require a little finessing; of course the rupture must come from her. There were things a man in his position had to be careful about. But with a direct suggestion—— Nothing was more obvious than that she did not care for him. He would make her say so. After that, a direct suggestion would be simple—and wholly justifiable. These were Mr. Lewis Ancram's reflections as he stood, hat in hand, on Mrs. Daye's landing. They were less involved than usual, but in equations of personal responsibility Mr. Ancram liked a formula. By the intelligent manipulation of a formula one could so often eliminate the personal element and transfer the responsibility to the other side.

The beginning was not auspicious.

"Is that *le dernier cri?*" he asked, looking at her hat as she came lightly down the steps.

"Papa's? Poor dear! yes. It was forty rupees, at Phelps's. You'll find me extravagant —but horribly!—especially in hats. I adore hats; they're such conceptions, such ideas! I mean to insist upon a settlement in hats—three every season, in perpetuity."

They were well into the street and half-way to Chowringhee before he found the remark, at which he forced himself to smile, that he supposed a time would arrive when her affections in millinery would transfer themselves to bonnets. The occasion was not propitious for suggestions based on emotional confessions. The broad roads that wind over the Maidan were full of gaiety and the definite facts of smart carriages and pretty bowing women. The sun caught the tops of the masts in the river, and twinkled there; it mellowed the pillars of the bathing-ghats, and was also reflected magnificently from the plate-glass mirrors with which Ram Das Mookerjee had adorned the sides of his barouche. A white patch a mile away resolved itself into a mass of black heads and draped bodies watching a cricket match. Mynas chattered by the wayside, stray notes of bugle practice came crisply over the walls of the Fort; there was an effect of cheerfulness even in the tinkle of the tram bells. If the scene had required any further touch of high spirits, it was supplied in the turn-out of the Maharajah of Thuginugger, who drove abroad in a purple velvet dressing gown, with pink outriders. Ancram had a fine susceptibility to atmospheric effect, and it bade him talk about the Maharajah of Thuginugger.

"That chap Ezra, the Simla diamond merchant, told me that he went with the Maharajah through his go-downs once. His Highness likes pearls. Ezra saw them standing about in bucketsful."

"Common wooden buckets?"

"I believe so."

"How satisfying! Tell me some more."

"There isn't any more. The rest was between Ezra and the Maharajah. I dare say there was a margin of profit somewhere. What queer weather they seem to be having at home!"

"It's delicious to live in a place that hasn't any weather—only a permanent fervency. I like this old Calcutta. It's so wicked and so rich and so cheerful. People are born and burned and born and burned, and nothing in the world matters. Their nice little stone gods are so easy to please, too. A handful of rice, a few marigold chains, a goat or two: hardly any of them ask more than that. And the sun shines every day —on the just man who has offered up his goat, and on the unjust man who has eaten it instead."

She sat up beside him, her slender figure swaying a little with the motion of the cart, and looked about her with a light in her grey eyes that seemed the reflection of her mood. He thought her chatter artificial; but it was genuine enough. She always felt more than her usual sense of irresponsibility with him in their afternoon drives. The world lay all about them and lightened their relation; he became, as a rule, the person who was driving, and she felt at liberty to become the person who was talking.

"There!" she exclaimed, as three or four coolie women filed, laughing, up to a couple of round stones under a pipal tree by the roadside, and took their brass lotas from their heads and carefully poured water over the stones. "Fancy one's religious obligations summed up in a cooking-potful of Hughli water! Are those stones sacred?"

"I suppose so."

"The author of 'The Modern Influence of the Vedic Books,'" she suggested demurely, "should be quite sure. He should have left no stone unturned."

She regarded him for a moment, and, observing his preoccupation, just perceptibly lifted her eyebrows. Then she went on: "But perhaps big round stones under pipal trees that like libations come in the second volume. When does the second volume appear?"

"Not until Sir Griffiths Spence comes out again and this lunatic goes back to Hassimabad, I fancy. I want an appropriation for some further researches first."

The most enthusiastic of Mr. Ancram's admirers acknowledged that he was not always discreet.

"And he won't give it to you—this lunatic?"

"Not a pice."

"Then," she said, with a ripple of laughter, "he *must* be a fool!"

She was certainly irritating this afternoon. Ancram gave his Waler as smart a cut as he dared, and they dashed past Lord Napier, sitting on his intelligent charger in serious bronze to all eternity, and rounded the bend into the Strand. The brown river tore at its heaving buoys; the tide was racing out. The sun had dipped, and the tall ships lay in the after-glow in twos and threes and congeries along the bank, along the edge of Calcutta, until in the curving distance they became mere suggestions of one another and a twilight of tilted masts. Under their keels slipped great breadths of shining water. Against the glow on it a country-boat, with its unwieldy load of hay, looked like a floating barn. On the indistinct other side the only thing that asserted itself was a factory chimney. They talked of the eternal novelty of the river, and the eternal sameness of the people they met; and then he lapsed again.

Rhoda looked down at the bow of her slipper. "Have you got a headache?" she asked. The interrogation was one of cheerful docility.

"Thanks, no. I beg your pardon: I'm afraid I was inexcusably preoccupied."

"Would it be indiscreet to ask what about? Don't you want my opinion? I am longing to give you my opinion."

"Your opinion would be valuable."

Miss Daye again glanced down at her slipper. This time her pretty eyelashes shaded a ray of amused perception. "He thinks he can do it himself," she remarked privately. "He is quite ready to give himself all the credit of getting out of it gracefully. The amount of flattery they demand for themselves, these Secretaries!"

"A premium on my opinion!" she said. "How delightful!"

Ancram turned the Waler sharply into the first road that led to the Casuerina Avenue. The Casuerina Avenue is almost always poetic, and might be imagined to lend itself very effectively, after sunset, to the funeral of a sentiment which Mr. Ancram was fond of describing to himself as still-born. The girl beside him noted the slenderness of his foot and the excellent cut of his grey tweed trousers. Her eyes dwelt upon the nervously vigorous way he handled the reins, and her glance of light bright inquiry ascertained a vertical line between his eyebrows. It was the line that accompanied the Honourable Mr. Ancram's Bills in Council, and it indicated a disinclination to compromise. Miss Daye, fully apprehending its significance, regarded him with an interest that might almost be described as affectionate. She said to herself that he would bungle. She was rather sorry for him. And he did.

"I should be glad of your opinion of our relation," he said—which was very crude.

"I think it is charming. I was never more interested in my life!" she declared frankly, bringing her lips together in the pretty composure with which she usually told the vague little lie of her satisfaction with life.

"Does that sum up your idea of—of the possibilities of our situation?" He felt that he was doing better.

"Oh no! There are endless possibilities in our situation—mostly stupid ones. But it is a most agreeable actuality."

"I wish," he said desperately, "that you would tell me just what the actuality means to you."

They were in the Avenue row, and the Waler had been allowed to drop into a walk. The after-glow still lingered in the soft green duskiness over their heads; there was light enough for an old woman to see to pick up the fallen spines in the grass; the nearest tank, darkling in the gathering gloom of the Maidan, had not yet given up his splash of red from over the river. He looked at her intently, and her eyes dropped to the thoughtful consideration of the crone who picked up spines. It might have been that she blushed, or it might have been some effect of the after-glow. Ancram inclined to the latter view, but his judgment could not be said to be impartial.

"Dear Lewis!" she answered softly, "how very difficult that would be!"

In the sudden silence that followed, the new creaking of the Waler's harness was perceptible. Ancram assured himself hotly that this was simple indecency, but it was a difficult thing to say. He was still guarding against the fatality of irritation when Rhoda added daintily:

"But I don't see why you should have a monopoly of catechising. Tell me, sir—I've wanted to know for ever so long—what was the first, the very first thing you saw in me to fall in love with?"

CHAPTER VII.

The Honourable Mr. Ancram's ideal policy toward the few score million subjects of the Queen-Empress for whose benefit he helped to legislate, was a paternalism somewhat highly tempered with the exercise of discipline. He had already accomplished appreciable things for their advantage, and he intended to accomplish more. It would be difficult to describe intelligibly all that he had done; besides, his tasks live in history. The publications of the Government of India hold them all, and something very similar may be found in the record which every retired civilian of distinction cherishes in leather, behind the glass of his bookcases in Brighton or Bournemouth. It would therefore be unnecessary as well.

It was Mr. Ancram's desire to be a conspicuous benefactor—this among Indian administrators is a matter of business, and must not be smiled at as a weakness—and in very great part he had succeeded. The fact should be remembered in connection with his expressed opinion—it has been said that he was not always discreet—that the relatives in the subordinate services of troublesome natives should be sent, on provocation, to the most remote and unpleasant posts in the province. To those who understand the ramifications of cousinly connection in the humbler service of the *sircar*, the detestation of exile and the claims of family affection in Bengal, the efficacy of this idea for promoting loyalty will appear. It was Mr. Ancram's idea, but he despaired of getting it adopted. Therefore he talked about it. Perhaps upon this charge he was not so very indiscreet after all.

It will be observed that Mr. Ancram's policy was one of exalted expediency. This will be even more evident when it is understood that, in default of the opportunity of coercing the subject Aryan for his highest welfare, Mr. Ancram conciliated him. The Chief Secretary had many distinguished native friends. They were always trying to make him valuable presents. When he returned the presents he did it in such a way that the bond of their mutual regard was cemented rather than otherwise—cemented by the tears of impulsive Bengali affection. He had other native friends who were more influential than distinguished. They spoke English and wrote it, most of them. They created the thing which is quoted in Westminster as "Indian Public Opinion." They were in the van of progress, and understood all the tricks for moving the wheels. The Government of India in its acknowledged capacity as brake found these gentlemen annoying; but Mr. Ancram, since he could not imprison them, offered them a measure of his sympathy. They quite understood that it was a small measure, but there is a fascination about the friendship of a Chief Secretary, and they often came to see him. They did not bring him presents, however; they knew very much better than that.

Mohendra Lall Chuckerbutty was one of these inconspicuously influential friends. Mohendra was not a maharajah: he was only a baboo, which stands, like "Mr." for hardly anything at all. To say that he was a graduate of the Calcutta University is to acknowledge very little; he was as clever before he matriculated as he was after he took his degree. But it should not be forgotten that he was the editor and proprietor of the *Bengal Free Press;* that was the distinction upon which, for the moment, he was insisting himself. The *Bengal Free Press* was a voice of the people—a particularly aggressive and pertinacious voice. It sold for two pice in the bazar, and was read by University students at the rate of twenty-five to each copy. It was regularly translated for the benefit of the Amir of Afghanistan, the Khan of Kelat, and such other people as were interested in knowing how insolent sedition could be in Bengal with safety; and it lay on the desk of every high official in the Province. Its advertisements were very funny, and its editorial English was more fluent than veracious: but when it threw mud at the Viceroy, and called the Lieutenant-

Governor a contemptible tyrant, and reminded the people that their galls were of the yoke of the stranger, there was no mistaking the direction of its sentiment.

Mohendra Lall Chuckerbutty sat in the room the Chief Secretary called his workshop, looking, in a pause of their conversation, at the Chief Secretary. No one familiar with that journal would have discovered in his amiable individuality the incarnation of the *Bengal Free Press*. On his head he wore a white turban, and on his countenance an expression of benign intelligence just tinged with uncertainty as to what to say next. His person was buttoned up to his perspiring neck in a tight black surtout, which represented his compromise with European fashions, and across its most pronounced rotundity hung a substantial gold watch-chain. From the coat downwards he fell away, so to speak, into Aryanism: the indefinite white draperies of his race were visible, and his brown hairy legs emerged from them bare. He had made progress, however, with his feet, on which he wore patent leather shoes, almost American in their neatness, with three buttons at the sides. He sat leaning forward a little, with his elbows on his knees, and his plump hands, their dimpled fingers spread apart, hanging down between them. Mohendra Lall Chuckerbutty's attitude expressed his very genuine anxiety to make the most of his visit.

Ancram leaned back in his tilted chair, with his feet on his desk, sharpening a lead pencil. "And that's my advice to you," he said, with his eyes on the knife.

"Well, I am grateful foritt! I am very much ob*liged* foritt!" Mohendra paused to relieve his nerves by an amiable, somewhat inconsequent laugh. "It iss my wish offcourse to be guided as far as possible by your opinion." Mohendra glanced deprecatingly at the matting. "But this is a *sir*rious grievance. And there are others who are always spikking with me and pushing me——"

"No grievance was ever mended in a day or a night, or a session, Baboo. Government moves slowly. Ref—changes are made by inches, not by ells. If you are wise, you'll be content with one inch this year and another next. It's the only way."

Mohendra smiled in sad agreement, and nodded two or three times, with his head rather on one side. It was an attitude so expressive of submission that the Chief Secretary's tone seemed unnecessarily decisive.

"The article on that admirable Waterways Bill off yours I hope you recivved. I sent isspecial marked copy."

"Yes," replied Ancram, in cordial admission: "I noticed it. Very much to the point. The writer thoroughly grasped my idea. Very grammatical too—and all that." Mr. Ancram yawned a little. "But you'd better keep my name out of your paper, Baboo—unless you want to abuse me. I'm a modest man, you know. That leader you speak of made me blush, I assure you."

It required all Mohendra's agility to arrive at the conclusion that if the Honourable Mr. Ancram really considered the influence of the *Bengal Free Press* of no importance, he would not take the trouble to say so. He arrived at it safely, though, while apparently he was only shaking his head and respectfully enjoying Mr. Ancram's humour, and saying, "Oh, no, no! If sometimes we blame, we must also often praise. Oh yess, certainlie. And *efery* one says it iss a good piece off work."

Ancram looked at his watch. The afternoon was mellowing. If Mohendra Lall Chuckerbutty had come for the purpose of discussing His Honour the Lieutenant-Governor's intentions towards the University Colleges, he had better begin. Mr. Ancram was aware that in so far as so joyous and auspicious an event as a visit to a Chief Secretary could be dominated by a purpose, Mohendra's was dominated by this one; and he had been for some time reflecting upon the extent to which he would allow himself to be drawn. He was at variance with John Church's administration—now that three months had made its direction manifest—at almost every point. He was at variance with John Church himself—that he admitted to be a matter of temperament. But Church had involved the Government of

Bengal in blunders from which the advice of his Chief Secretary, if he had taken it, would have saved him. He had not merely ignored the advice: he had rejected it somewhat pointedly, being a candid man and no diplomat. If he had acknowledged his mistakes ever so privately, his Chief Secretary would have taken a fine ethical pleasure in forgiving them; but the Lieutenant-Governor appeared to think that where principle was concerned the consideration of expediency was wholly superfluous, and continued to defend them instead, even after he could plainly see, in the *Bengal Free Press* and elsewhere, that they had begun to make him unpopular. Ancram's vanity had never troubled him till now. It had grown with his growth, and strengthened with his strength, under the happiest circumstances, and he had been as little aware of it as of his arterial system. John Church had made him unpleasantly conscious of it, and he was as deeply resentful as if John Church had invested him with it. The Honourable Mr. Ancram had never been discounted before, and that this experience should come to him through an official superior whom he did not consider his equal in many points of administrative sagacity, was a circumstance that had its peculiar irritation. Mohendra Lall Chuckerbutty was very well aware of this; and yet he did not feel confident in approaching the matter of His Honour and the higher culture. It was a magnificent grievance. Mohendra had it very much at heart, the *Free Press* would have it very much at heart, and nothing was more important than the private probing of the Chief Secretary's sentiment regarding it; yet Mohendra hesitated. He wished very much that there were some tangible reason why Ancram should take sides against the Lieutenant-Governor, some reason that could be expressed in rupees: then he would have had more confidence in hoping for an adverse criticism. But for a mere dislike, a mere personal antagonism, it would be so foolish. Thus Mohendra vacillated, stroking his fat cheek with his fingers, and looking at the matting. Ancram saw that his visitor would end by abandoning his intention, and became aware that he would prefer that this should not happen.

"And what do you think," he said casually, "of our proposal to make you all pay for your Greek?"

Mohendra beamed. "I think, sir, that it cannot be *your* proposal."

"It isn't," said Ancram sententiously.

"If it becomes law, it will be the signal for a great disturbance. I mean, off course," the Baboo hastened to add, "of a pa*cific* kind. No violence, of course! Morally speaking the community is already up in arms—*morally* speaking! It is destructive legislation, sir; we *must* protest."

"I don't blame you for that."

"Then you do not yourself approve off it?"

"I think it's a mistake. Well-intentioned, but a mistake."

"Oh, the *intention*, that iss good! But impracticable," Mohendra ventured vaguely: "a bubble in the air—that is all; but the question i—iz," he went on, "will it become law? Yesterday only I first heard offitt. Mentally I said,

'I will go to my noble friend and find out for myself the rights offitt!' *Then* I will act."

"Oh, His Honour intends to put it through. If you mean to do anything there's no time to lose." Ancram assured himself afterwards that between his duty as an administrator and his private sentiment toward his chief there could be no choice.

"We will petition the Viceroy."

Ancram shook his head. "Time wasted. The Viceroy will stick to Church."

"Then we can petition the Secretary-off-State."

"That might be useful, if you get the right names."

"We will have it fought out in Parliament. Mr. Dadabhai——"

"Yes," Ancram responded with a smile, "Mr. Dadabhai——"

"There will be mass meetings on the Maidan."

"Get them photographed and send them to the *Illustrated London News*."

"And every paper will be agitating it. The

Free Press the *Hindu Patriot*, the *Bengalee*—all offthem will be writing about it——"

"There is one thing you must remember if the business goes to England—the converts of these colleges from which State aid is to be withdrawn."

"Christians?" Mohendra shook his head with a smile of contempt. "There are none. It iss not to change their religion that the Hindus go to college."

"Ah!" returned Ancram. "There are none? That is a pity. Otherwise you might have got them photographed too, for the illustrated papers."

"Yes. It iss a pity."

Mohendra reflected profoundly for a moment. "But I will remember what you say about the fottograff—if any can be found."

"Well, let me know how you get on. In my private capacity—in my *private* capacity, remember—as the friend and well-wisher of the people, I shall be interested in what you do. Of course I talk rather freely to you, Baboo, because we know each other well. I have not concealed my opinion in this matter at any time, but for all that it mustn't be known that I have active sympathies. You understand. This is entirely confidential."

" Oh, offcourse! my gracious goodness, yes!"

Mohendra's eyes were moist—with gratification. He was still trying to express it when he withdrew, ten minutes later, backing toward the door. Ancram shut it upon him somewhat brusquely, and sent a servant for a whisky-and-soda. It could not be said that he was in the least nervous, but he was depressed. It always depressed him to be compelled to take up an attitude which did not invite criticism from every point of view. His present attitude had one aspect in which he was compelled to see himself driving a nail into the acting Lieutenant-Governor's political coffin. Ancram would have much preferred to see all the nails driven in without the necessity for his personal assistance. His reflections excluded Judith Church as completely as if the matter were no concern of hers. He considered her separately. The strengthening of the bond between them was a pleasure which had detached itself from all the other interests of his life; he thought of it tenderly, but the tenderness was rather for his sentimental property in her than for her in any material sense. She stood, with the dear treasure of her sympathy, apart from the Calcutta world, and as far apart from John Church as from the rest.

That evening, at dinner, Ancram told Philip Doyle and another man that he had been drawing Mohendra Lall Chuckerbutty on the University College question, and he was convinced that feeling was running very high.

"The fellow had the cheek to boast about the row they were going to make," said Mr. Ancram.

CHAPTER VIII.

PHILIP DOYLE did not know at all how it was that he found himself at the Maharajah of Pattore's garden-party. He had not the honour of knowing the Maharajah of Pattore—his invitation was one of the many amiabilities which he declared he owed to his distinguished connection with the Bengal Secretariat in the person of Lewis Ancram. Certainly Ancram had asked him to accept, and take his, Ancram's, apologies to the Maharajah; but that seemed no particular reason why he should be there. The fact was, Doyle assured himself, as he bowled along through the rice-fields of the suburbs to His Highness's garden-house—the fact was, he was restless, he needed change supremely, and anything out of the common round had its value. Things in Calcutta had begun to wear an unusually hard and irritating look; he felt his eye for the delinquencies of human nature growing keener and more critical. This state of things, taken in connection with the possession of an undoubted sense of humour, Doyle recognised to be grave. He told himself that, although he was unaware of anything actually physically wrong, the effects of the climate were most insidious, and he made it a subject of congratulation that his passage was taken in the *Oriental*.

There was a festival arch over the gate when he reached it, and a multitude of little flags, and "WELLCOME" pendent in yellow marigolds. Doyle was pleased that he had come. It was a long time since he had attended a Maharajah's garden party; its features would be fresh and in some ways soothing. He shook hands gravely with the Maharajah's eldest son, a slender, subdued, cross-eyed young man in an embroidered smoking-cap and a purple silk frock-coat, and said "Thank you—thank you!" for a programme of the afternoon's diversions. The programme was printed in gold letters, and he was glad to learn from it that His Highness's country residence was called " Floral Bower." This was entirely as it should be. He noticed that the Maharajah had provided wrestling and dancing and theatricals for the amusement of his guests, and resolved to see them all. He had a pleasant sense of a strain momentarily removed, and he did not importune himself to explain it. There were very few English people in the crowd that flocked about the grounds, following with docile admiration the movements of the principal guests; it was easy to keep away from them. He had only to stroll about, and look at the curiously futile arrangement of ponds and grottoes and fountains and summer-houses, and observe how pretty a rose-bush could be in spite of everything and how appropriately brilliant the clothes of the Maharajah's friends were. Some of the younger ones were playing football, with much laughter and screaming and wonderfully high kicks. He stood and watched them, smilingly reflecting that he would back a couple of Harrovians against the lot. His eyes were still on the boys and the smile was still on his lips when he found himself considering that he would reach England just about the day of Ancram's wedding. Then he realised that Ancram's wedding had for him some of the characteristics of a physical ailment which one tries, by forgetting, to conjure out of existence. The football became less amusing, and he was conscious that much of its significance had faded out of the Maharajah's garden-party. Nevertheless he followed the feebly curved path which led to His Highness's private menagerie, and it was while he was returning the unsympathetic gaze of a very mangy tiger in a very ramshackle cage, that the reflection came between them, as forcibly as if it were a new one, that he would come back next cold weather to an empty house. Ancram would be married. He acknowledged, still carefully examining the tiger, that he would regret the man less if his departure were due to any other reason; and he tried to determine, without much success, to what extent he could blame himself in that his liking for Ancram had dwindled so considerably during the last few months. By the time he turned his back upon the zoölogical attraction of the afternoon he had fallen into the reverie from which he hoped to escape in the *Oriental*—the recollection, perfect in every detail, of the five times he had met Rhoda Daye before her engagement, and a little topaz necklace she had worn three times out of the five, and the several things that he wished he had said, and especially the agreeable exaltation of spirit in which he had called himself, after every one of these interviews, an elderly fool.

His first thought when he saw her, a moment after, walking towards him with her father, was of escape—the second quickened his steps in her direction, for she had bowed, and after that there could be no idea of going. He concluded later, with definiteness, that it would have been distinctly rude when there were not more than twenty Europeans in the place. Colonel Daye's solid white-whiskered countenance broke into a square smile as Doyle approached—a smile which expressed that it was rather a joke to meet a friend at a maharajah's garden party.

"You're a singular being," he said, as they shook hands; "one never comes across you in the haunts of civilisation. Here's *my* excuse."

Colonel Daye indicated his daughter. " Would come. Offered to take her to the races instead—wouldn't look at it!"

"If I had no reason for coming before, I've found one," said Doyle, with an inclination towards Rhoda that laid the compliment at her feet. There were some points about Philip Doyle that no emotional experience could altogether subdue. He would have said precisely the same thing, with precisely the same twinkle, to any woman he liked.

Rhoda looked at him gravely, having no response ready. If the in-drawing of her under-lip betrayed anything it was that she felt the least bit hurt—which, in Rhoda Daye, was ridiculous. If she had been asked she might have explained it by the fact that there were people whom she preferred to take her seriously, and in the ten seconds during which her eyes questioned this politeness she grew gradually delicately pink under his.

"Rum business, isn't it?" Colonel Daye went on, tapping the backs of his legs with his stick. "Hallo! there's Grigg. I must see Grigg—do you mind? Don't wait, you know—just walk on. I'll catch you up in ten minutes."

Without further delay Colonel Daye joined Grigg.

"That's like my father," said the girl, with a trace of embarrassment: "he never can resist the temptation of disposing of me, if it's only for ten minutes. We ought to feel better acquainted than we do. I've been out seven months now, but it is still only before people that we dare to chaff each other. I think," she added, turning her grey eyes seriously upon Doyle, "that he finds it awkward to have so much of the society of a young lady who requires to be entertained."

"What a pity that is!" Doyle said involuntarily.

She was going to reply with one of her bright, easy cynicisms, and then for some reason changed her mind. "I don't know about the advantage of very deep affections," she said involuntarily, and there was no flippancy in her tone. Doyle fancied that he detected a note of pathos instead, but perhaps he was looking for it.

They were walking with a straggling company of baboos in white muslin down a double row of plantains towards the wrestling ring. Involuntarily he made their pace slower.

"You can't be touched by that ignoble spirit of the age—already."

Miss Daye felt her moral temperature fall several degrees from the buoyant condition in which she contrived to keep it as a rule. To say she experienced a chill in the region of her conscience is perhaps to put it grotesquely, but she certainly felt inclined to ask Philip Doyle with some astonishment what difference it made to him.

"The spirit of the age is an annoying thing. It robs one of all originality."

"Pray," he said, "be original in some other direction. You have a very considerable choice."

His manner disarmed his words. It was grave, almost pleading. She wondered why she was not angry, but the fact remained that she was only vaguely touched, and rather unhappy. Then he spoiled it.

"In my trade we get into dogmatic ways," he apologised. "You won't mind the carpings of an elderly lawyer who has won a bad eminence for himself by living for twenty years in Calcutta. By the way, I had Ancram's apologies to deliver to the Maharajah. If he had known he would perhaps have entrusted me with more important ones." Doyle made this speech in general compensation, to any one who wanted it, for being near her—with her. If he expected blushing confusion he failed to find it.

"He didn't know," she said indifferently; "and if he had—— Oh, there are the wrestlers." She looked at them for a moment with disfavour. "Do you like them? I think they are like performing animals."

The men separated for a moment and rubbed their shining brown bodies with earth. Somewhere near the gate the Maharajah's band struck up "God Save the Queen," four prancing pennons appeared over the tops of the bushes, and with one accord the crowd moved off in that direction. A moment later His Highness was doubling up in appreciation of His Excellency's condescension in arriving. His Excellency himself was surrounded ten feet deep by his awestruck and delighted fellow-guests, and the wrestlers, bereft of an audience, sat down and spat.

What Doyle always told himself that he must do with regard to Miss Daye was to approach her in the vein of polished commonplace—polished because he owed it to himself, commonplace because its after effect on the nerves he found to be simpler. Realising his departure from this prescribed course, he fervently set himself down a hectoring idiot, and looked round for Colonel Daye. Colonel Daye radiated the commonplace; he was a most usual person. In his society there was not the slightest danger of saying anything embarrassing. But he was not even remotely visible.

"Believe me," said Rhoda, with sudden divination, "we shall be lucky if we see my father again in half an hour. I am very sorry, but he really is a most unnatural parent." There was a touch of defiance in her laugh. He should not lecture her again. "Where shall we go?"

"Have you seen the acting?"

"Yes. It's a conversation between Rama

and Shiva. Rama wears a red wig and Shiva wears a yellow one; the rest is tinsel and pink muslin. They sit on the floor and argue—that is the play. While one argues the other chews betel and looks at the audience. I've seen better acting," she added demurely, "at the Corinthian Theatre."

Doyle laughed irresistibly. Calcutta's theatrical resources, even in the season, lend themselves to frivolous suggestion.

"I could show you the Maharajah's private chapel, if you like," she said.

Doyle replied that nothing could be more amusing than a Maharajah's private chapel; and as they walked together among the rose bushes he felt every consideration, every scruple almost, slip away from him in the one desire her nearness always brought him—the desire for that kind of talk with her which should seal the right he vaguely knew was his to be acknowledged in a privacy of her soul that was barred against other people. Once or twice before he had seemed almost to win it, and by some gay little saying which rang false upon his sincerity she had driven him back. She assuredly did not seem inclined to give him an opportunity this afternoon. It must be confessed that she chattered, in that wilful, light, irrelevant way that so stimulated his desire to be upon tenderly serious terms with her, by no means as her mentor, but for his own satisfaction and delight. She chattered, with her sensitiveness alive at every point to what he should say and to what she thought she could guess he was thinking. She believed him critical, which was distressing in view of her conviction that he could never understand her—never! He belonged to an older school, to another world; his feminine ideal was probably some sister or mother, with many virtues and no opinions. He was a person to respect and admire—she did respect and she did admire him—but to expect any degree of fellowship from him was absurd. The incomprehensible thing was that this conclusion should have any soreness about it. For the moment she was not aware that this was so; her perception of it had a way of coming afterwards, when she was alone.

"Here it is," she said, at the entrance of a little grotto made of stucco and painted to look like rock, serving no particular purpose, by the edge of an artificial lake. "And here is the shrine and the divinity!"

As a matter of fact, there was a niche in the wall, and the niche held Hanuman with his monkey face and his stolen pineapple, coy in painted plaster.

Miss Daye looked at the figure with a crisp assumption of interest. "Isn't he amusing!" she remarked: "'Bloomin' idol made o' mud'!"

"And so this is where you think His Highness comes to say his prayers?" Doyle said, smiling.

"Perhaps he has a baboo to say them for him," she returned, as they strolled out. "That would be an ideal occupation for a baboo—to make representations on behalf of one exalted personage to another. I wonder what he asks Hanuman for! To be protected from all the evils of this life, and to wake up in the next another maharajah!"

He was so engaged with the airiness of her

whimsicality and the tilt of the feather in her hat that he found no answer ready for this, and to her imagination he took the liberty of disapproving her flippancy. Afterwards she told herself that it was not a liberty—that the difference in their ages made it a right if he chose to take it—but at the moment the idea incited her to deepen his impression. She cast about her for the wherewithal to make the completest revelation of her cheaper qualities. In a crisis of candour she would show him just how audacious and superficial and trivial she could be. Women have some curious instincts.

"I am dying," she said, with vivacity, "to see how His Highness keeps house. They say he has a golden chandelier and the prettiest harem in Bengal. And I confide to you, Mr. Doyle, that I should like a glass of simpkin —immensely. It goes to my head in the most amusing way in the middle of the afternoon."

"His ideal young woman," she declared to herself, "would have said 'champagne'—no, she would have preferred tea; and she would have died rather than mention the harem."

But it must be confessed that Philip Doyle was more occupied for the moment with the curve of her lips than with anything that came out of them, except in so far that everything she said seemed to place him more definitely at a distance.

"I'm afraid," he returned, "that the ladies are all under double lock and key for the occasion, but there ought to be no difficulty about the champagne and the chandelier."

At that moment Colonel Daye's tall grey hat came into view, threading the turbaned crowd in obvious quest. Rhoda did not see it, and Doyle immediately found a short cut to the house which avoided the encounter. He had suddenly remembered several things that he wanted to say. They climbed a flight of marble stairs covered with some dirty yards of matting, and found themselves almost alone in the Maharajah's drawing-room. The Viceroy had partaken of an ice and gone down again, taking the occasion with him; and the long table at the end of the room was almost as heavily laden as when the confectioner had set it forth.

"A little pink cake in a paper boat, please," she commanded, "with jam inside"; and then, as Doyle went for it, she sat down on one of Pattore's big brocaded sofas, and crossed her pretty feet, and looked at the chromolithographs of the Prince and Princess of Wales askew upon the wall, and wondered why she was making a fool of herself.

"I've brought you a cup of coffee: do you mind?" he asked, coming back with it. "His Highness' intentions are excellent, but the source of his supplies is obscure. I tried the champagne," he added apologetically: "it's unspeakable!"

No, Miss Daye did not mind. Doyle sat down at the other end of the sofa, and reflected that another quarter of an hour was all he could possibly expect, and then——

"I am going home, Miss Daye," he said.

Since there was no other way of introducing himself to her consideration, he would do it with a pitchfork.

"I knew you were. Soon?"

"The day after to-morrow, in the *Oriental.* I suppose Ancram told you?"

"I believe he did. You and he are great friends, aren't you?"

"We live together. Men must be able to tolerate each other pretty fairly to do that."

"How long shall you be in England?"

"Six months, I hope."

She was silent, and he fancied she was thinking, with natural resentment, that he might have postponed his departure until after the wedding. Doyle hated a lie more than most people, but he felt the situation required that he should say something.

"The exigency of my going is unkind," he blundered. "It will deprive me of the pleasure of offering Ancram my congratulations."

There was only the faintest flavour of mendacity about this; but she detected it, and fitted it, with that unerring feminine instinct we hear so much about, to her thought. For an instant she seemed lost in buttoning her glove; then she looked up, with a little added colour.

"Don't tamper with your sincerity for me," she said quickly: "I'm not worth it. It's very kind of you to consider my feelings, but I would much rather have the plain truth between us—that you don't approve of me or of the—the marriage. I jar upon you—oh! I see it! a dozen times in half an hour—and you are sorry for your friend. For his sake you even try to like me: I've seen you doing it. Please don't: it distresses me to know that you take that trouble——"

"Here you are!" exclaimed Colonel Daye, in the doorway. "Much obliged to you, Doyle, really, for taking care of this little girl. Most difficult man to get hold of, Grigg."

CHAPTER IX.

It has been obvious, I hope, that Lewis Ancram was temperamentally equal to adjusting himself to a situation. His philosophy was really characteristic of him; and none the less so because it had a pessimistic and artistic tinge, and he wore it in a Persian motto inside a crest ring on his little finger. It can hardly be said that he adjusted himself to his engagement and his future, when it became apparent to him that the one could not be broken or the other changed, with cheerfulness—for cheerfulness was too commonplace a mental condition to have characterised Mr. Ancram under the happiest circumstances. Neither can it be denied, however, that he did it with a good deal of dignity and some tact. He permitted himself to lose the abstraction that had been overcoming him so habitually in Rhoda's society, and he said more of those clever things to her which had been temporarily obscured by the cloud on his spirits. They saw one another rather oftener than usual in the fortnight following the evening on which Mr. Ancram thought he could suggest a course for their mutual benefit to Miss Daye and her daintily authoritative manner with him convinced him that his chains were riveted very firmly. At times he told himself that she had, after all, affectionate potentialities, though he met the problem of evolving them with a shrug. He disposed himself to accept all the ameliorations of the situation that were available, all the consolations he could find. One of the subtlest and therefore most appreciable of these was the necessity, which his earlier confidence involved, of telling Judith Church in a few suitably hesitating and well-chosen words that things were irrevocable. Judith kept silence for a moment, and then, with a gravely impersonal smile, she said, "I hope—and think—you may be happier than you expect," in a manner which made further discussion of the matter impossible. It cannot be doubted, however, that she was able to convey to him an under-current of her sympathy without embarrassment. Otherwise he would hardly have found himself so dependent on the odd half-hours during which they talked of Henley's verses and Swan's pictures and the possibility of barricading oneself against the moral effect of India. Ancram often gave her to understand, in one delicate way or another, that if there were a few more women like her in the country it could be done.

The opinion seemed to be general, though perhaps nobody else formulated it exactly in those terms. People went about assuring each other that Mrs. Church was the most charming social success, asserting this as if they recognised that it was somewhat unusual to confer such a decoration upon a lady whose husband had as yet none whatever. People said she was a really fascinating woman in a manner which at once condoned and suggested her undistinguished antecedents—an art which practice has made perfect in the bureaucratic circles of India. They even went so far as to add that the atmosphere of Belvedere had entirely changed since the beginning of the officiating period—which was preposterous, for nothing could change the social atmosphere of any court of Calcutta short of the reconstruction of the Indian Empire. The total of this meant that Mrs. Church had a good memory, much considerateness, an agreeable disposition, and pretty clothes. Her virtues, certainly her virtues as I know them, would hardly be revealed in the fierce light which beats upon the wife of an acting Lieutenant-Governor of Bengal from November until April, though a shadow of one of them might have been detected in the way she behaved to the Dayes. Ancram thought her divine in this, but she was only an honest woman with a temptation and a scruple. Her dignity made it difficult; she was obliged to think out delicate little ways of offering them her friendship in the scanty half hours she had to herself after dinner, while the unending scratch of her husband's pen came through the portière that hung across the doorway into his dressing-room. What she could do without consulting them she did; though it is not likely that Colonel Daye will ever attribute the remarkable smoothness of his official path at this time to anything but the spirit of appreciation in which he at last found Government disposed to regard his services. The rest was not so easy, because she had to count with Rhoda. On this point her mother was in the habit of invoking Rhoda's better nature, with regrettable futility. Mrs. Daye said that for her part she accepted an invitation in the spirit in which it was given, and it is to be feared that no lady in Mrs. Church's "official position" would be compelled to make overtures twice to Mrs. Daye, who told other ladies, in confidence, that she had the best reason to believe Mrs. Church a noble-minded woman—a beautiful soul. It distressed her that she was not able to say this to Rhoda also, to be frank with Rhoda, to discuss the situation and perhaps to hint to the dear child that her non-responsiveness to Mrs. Church's very kind attitude looked "the least bit in the world like the little green monster, you know, dearest one." It was not, Mrs. Daye acknowledged, that Rhoda actively resisted Mrs. Church's interest; she simply appeared to be unaware of it, and sat on a chair beside that sweet woman in the Belvedere drawing-room with the effect of being a hundred miles away. Mrs. Daye sometimes asked herself apprehensively how soon Mrs. Church would grow tired of coaxing Rhoda, how long their present beatitudes might be expected to last. It was with this consideration in mind that she went to her daughter's room the day after the Maharajah of Pattore's garden-party, which was Thursday. The windows of that apartment were wide open, letting in great squares of vivid sunlight, and their muslin curtains bellied inward with the pleasant north wind. It brought gusts of sound from the life outside—the high plaintive cheeling of the kites, the interminable cawing of the crows, the swish of the palm fronds, the scolding of the mynas; and all this life and light and clamour seemed to centre in and circle about the yellow-haired girl who sat, half-dressed, on the edge of the bed writing a letter. She laid it aside face downward, at her mother's knock, and that amiable lady found her daughter seated before the looking-glass with a crumpled little brown ayah brushing her hair.

Mrs. Daye cried out at the glare, at the noise. "It's like living in one of those fretwork marble summer-houses at Delhi where the kings of what-you-may-call-it dynasty kept their wives!" she declared, with her hands pressed on her eyes and a thumb in each ear; and when the shutters were closed and the room reduced to some degree of tranquillity, broken by glowing points where the green slats came short of the sash, she demanded eau-de-cologne and sank into a chair. "I've come for 'Cruelle Enigme,' Rhoda," Mrs. Daye announced.

"No, you haven't, mummie. And besides, you can't have it—it isn't a nice book for you to read."

"Can't I?" Mrs. Daye asked plaintively. "Well, dear, I suppose I must take your opinion —you know how much my wretched nerves will stand. From all I hear I certainly can't be too thankful to you for protecting me from Zola."

"Ayah," Rhoda commanded in the ayah's tongue, "give me the yellow book on the little table—the yellow one, owl's daughter! Here's one you can have, mother," she said, turning over a few of the leaves with a touch that was a caress—"'Robert Helmont'—you haven't read that."

Mrs. Daye glanced at it without enthusiasm.

"It's about a war, isn't it? I'm not fond of books about wars as a rule, they're so 'bluggy,'" and the lady made a little face; "but of course—oh yes, Daudet, I know he would be charming even if he *was* bluggy. Rhoda, don't make any engagement for Sunday afternoon. I've accepted an invitation from Belvedere for a river-party."

The face in the looking-glass showed the least contraction between the eyebrows. The ayah saw it, and brushed even more gently than before. Mrs. Daye was watching for it, and hurried on. "I gather from Mrs. Church's extremely kind note—she writes herself, and not the aide-de-camp—that it is a little *fête* she is making especially, in a manner, for you and Mr. Ancram, dear—in celebration, as it were. She has asked only people we know very well indeed; it is really almost a family affair. *Very sweet of her I call it, though of course Lewis*

Ancram is an old friend of—of the Lieutenant-Governor's."

The contraction between the girl's brows deepened seriously, gave place to a considering air, and for a moment she looked straight into her own eyes in the glass and said nothing. They rewarded her presently with a bubble of mischievous intelligence, which almost broke into a smile. Mrs. Daye continued to the effect that nothing did one so much good as a little jaunt on the river—it seemed to blow the malaria out of one's system—for her part she would give up anything for it. But Rhoda had no other engagement?

"Oh dear no!" Miss Daye replied. "There is nothing in the world to interfere!"

"Then you will go, dearest one?"

"I shall be delighted."

"My darling child, you *have* relieved my mind! I was so afraid that some silly little fad—I know how much you dislike the glare of the river——" then, forgetfully, "I will write at once and accept for us all." Mrs. Daye implanted a kiss upon her daughter's forehead, with a sense that she was picturesquely acknowledging dutiful obedience, and rustled out. "Robert Helmont" remained on the floor beside her chair, and an indefinitely pleasant freshness was diffused where she had been.

As Rhoda twisted her hair a little uncontrollable smile came to her lips and stayed there. "Ayah, worthy one," she said, "give me the letter from the bed"; and having read what she had written she slowly tore it into very small pieces. "After all," she reflected, "that would be a stupid way."

CHAPTER X.

THE opinion was a united one on board the *Annie Laurie* the next Sunday afternoon that Nature had left nothing undone to make the occasion a success. This might have testified to less than it did; for a similar view has been expressed as unanimously, and adhered to as firmly, on board the *Annie Laurie* when the banks of the Hooghly have been grey with deluge and the ladies have saved their skirts by sitting on one another's knees in her tiny cabin. The *Annie Laurie* being the Lieutenant-Governor's steam-launch, nobody but the Lieutenant-Governor presumes to be anything but complimentary as to the weather experienced aboard her. And this in India is natural. It could not be said, however, that there was anything necessarily diplomatic even in Mrs. Daye's appreciation of this particular afternoon. The air—they all dilated on the air—blew in from the sea, across the salt marshes, through the plantains and the cocoanut-trees of the little villages, and brought a dancing crispness, softened by the sun. The brown river hurtled outwards past her buoys, and a great merchant ship at anchor in midstream swung slowly round with the tide. A vague concourse of straight masts and black hulls and slanting funnels stretched along the bank behind them with the indefiniteness that comes of multitude, for every spar and line stood and swung clear cut in the glittering sun; and the point they were bound for elbowed itself out into the river two miles farther down, in the grey greenness of slanting, pluming palms. Already the water was growing more golden where the palms toppled over the river: there would not be more than two good hours of daylight. As Mrs. Daye remarked to the Lieutenant-Governor, life was all too short in the cold weather really to absorb, to drink in, the beauties of nature—there was so much going on.

"Then," said His Honour, "we must make the most of our time." But he did not prolong his gaze at Mrs. Daye by way of emphasising his remark, as another man, and especially another lieutenant-governor, might have done. He fixed it instead on the dilapidated plaster façade on the left bank of the river, formerly inhabited by the King of Oudh and his relatives, and thought of the deplorable sanitation there.

Not that John Church was by any means unappreciative of the beauties of nature. It was because he acknowledged the moral use of them that he came on these Sunday afternoon picnics. He read the poets, and would pay a good price for a bronze or a picture, for much the same reason. They formed part of his system of self-development; he applied them to his mind through the medium which nature has provided, and trusted that the effect would be good. He did it, however, as he did everything, with the greatest possible economy of time, and sometimes other considerations overlapped. That very afternoon he meant to speak to the Superintendent of the Botanical Gardens—the green elbow of the river crooked about this place—concerning the manufacture and distribution of a new febrifuge, and he presently edged away from Mrs. Daye with the purpose of finding out her husband's views concerning the silting up of river-beds in Bengal and the cost of preventive measures. Life with John Church could be measured simply as an area for effort.

Notwithstanding these considerations, it was gay enough. Captain Thrush, A.D.C., sat on the top of the cabin, and swung his legs to the accompaniment of his amusing experiences the last time he went quail shooting. The St. Georges were there, and the St. Georges were proverbial in Calcutta for lightheartedness. Sir William Scott might have somewhat overweighted the occasion; but Sir William Scott had taken off his hat, the better to enjoy the river-breeze, and this reduced him to a name and a frock coat. In the general good spirits the abnegation and the resolution with which Lewis Ancram and Judith Church occupied themselves with other people might almost have passed unnoticed. Rhoda Daye found herself wondering whether it would be possible for Ancram to be pathetic under the most moving circumstances, so it may be pre-

Notwithstanding, it was gay enough.

sumed that she perceived it; but the waves of mirth engendered by Captain Thrush and the St. Georges rolled over it so far as the rest were concerned, as they might over a wreck of life and hope. This pretty simile occurred to Miss Daye, who instantly dismissed it as mawkish, but nevertheless continued, for at least five minutes, to reflect on the irony of fate, as, for the moment, she helped to illustrate it. A new gravity fell upon her for that period, as she sat there and watched Judith Church talking to Sir William Scott about his ferns. For the first time she became aware that the situation had an edge to it—that she was the edge. She was the saturnine element in what she had hitherto resolutely regarded as a Calcutta comedy; she was not sure that she could regard it as a comedy any longer, even from the official point of view. Ancram evidently had it in mind to make an exhibition to the world in general, and to Mrs. Church in particular, of devotion to his betrothed. She caught him once or twice in the act of gratefully receiving Mrs. Church's approving glance. Nevertheless she had an agreeable tolerance for all that he found to do for her. She forbade herself, for the time being, any further analysis of a matter with which she meant to have in future little concern. In that anticipation she became unaccountably light-hearted and talkative and merry. So much so, that Captain Thrush, A.D.C., registered his conviction that she was really rather a pretty girl—more in her than he thought; and the Honourable Mr. Lewis Ancram said to himself that she was enjoying, in anticipation, the prestige she would have a month later, and that the cleverest of women were deplorably susceptible to social ambition.

The Superintendent met them at the wharf, and John Church led the way up the great central avenue of palms, whose grey, shaven polls look as if they had been turned by some giant lathe, with his hand on the arm of this gentleman. The others arranged themselves with a single eye to avoiding the stupidity of walking with their own wives and trooped after.

"We are going to the orchid-houses, John," Mrs. Church called after her husband, as Sir

William Scott brought them to a halt at a divergent road he loved; and Church took off his hat in hurried acquiescence.

"Notice my new Dendrobium!" cried the Superintendent, turning a rueful countenance upon them. "The only one in Asia!" Then his head resumed its inclination of respectful attention, and the pair disappeared.

Mrs. Church laughed frankly. "Poor Dr. James!" she exclaimed. "My husband is double-dyed in febrifuge to-day."

Ancram took the privilege—it was one he enjoyed—of gently rebuking her. "It is one of those common, urgent needs of the people," he said, "that His Honour so intimately understands."

Judith looked at him with a sudden sweet humility in her eyes. "You are quite right," she returned. "I sometimes think that nobody knows him as you do. Certainly," she added, in a lower tone, as the two fell back, "nobody has more of his confidence, more of his dependence."

"I don't know," Ancram answered vaguely. "Do you really think so? I don't know."

"I am sure of it."

He looked straight before him in silence, irritated in his sensitive morality—the morality which forbade him to send a Government *chuprassie* on a private errand, or to write to his relations in England on office paper. A curve in the walk showed them Rhoda Daye, standing alone on the sward, beside a bush in crimson-and-orange flower, intently examining a spray. Almost involuntarily they paused, and Ancram turned his eyes upon Mrs. Church with the effect of asking her what he should do, what he must do.

"Go!" she said; and then, as if it were a commonplace: "I think Miss Daye wants you. I will overtake the others."

She thought he left her very willingly, and hurried on with the conviction that, like everything else, it would come right—quite right—in the end. She was very happy if in any way she had helped it to come right—so happy that she longed to be alone with her sensations, and revolted with all her soul against the immediate necessity of Sir William Scott and the St. Georges. To be for a few hours quite alone, unseen and unknown, in the heart of some empty green wilderness like this, would help her, she knew, to rationalise her satisfaction. "My dear boy," she said, with nervous patience, as Captain Thrush appeared in search of her, "did you think I had fallen into a tank? Do go and take care of the other people." An aide-de-camp was not a serious impediment to reflection, but at the moment Judith would have been distressed by the attendance of her own shadow, if it were too perceptible.

Ancram crossed over to Rhoda, with his antipathy to the Lieutenant-Governor sensibly aggravated by the fact that his wife took an interest in him—an appreciative interest. It was out of harmony, Ancram felt vaguely, that she should do this—it jarred. He had so admired her usual attitude of pale, cool, sweet tolerance toward John Church—had so approved it. That attitude had been his solace in thinking about her in her unique position and with her rare temperament. To suppose her counting up her husband's virtues, weighing them, doing justice to them, tinged her with the commonplace, and disturbed him.

"That's a curious thing," he said to Rhoda.

She let go her hold of the twig, and the red-and-gold flower danced up like a flame.

"It belongs to the sun and the soil; so it pleases one better than any importation."

"An orchid is such a fairy—you can't expect it to have a nationality," he returned.

She stood, with her head thrown back a little, looking at the sprays that swung above the line of her lips. Her wide-brimmed hat dropped a soft shadow over the upper part of her face; her eyes shone through it with a gleam of intensely feminine sweetness, and the tender curve of her throat gave him an unreasoned throb of anticipation. In six weeks he would be married to this slender creature; it would be an excursion into the unknown, not unaccompanied by adventures. Tentatively, it might be agreeable; it would certainly be interesting. He confessed to a curiosity which was well on the way to become impatient.

"Then do you want to go and see the Dendrobium?" she asked.

"Not if you prefer to do anything else."

"I think I would enjoy the cranes more, or the pink water-lilies. The others will understand, won't they, that we two might like to take a little walk?"

Her coquetry, he said to himself, was preposterously pretty. They took another of the wide solitary paths that led under showery bamboos and quivering mahogany trees to where a stretch of water gave back the silence of the palms against the evening sky, and he dropped unconsciously into the stroll which is characterised everywhere as a lover's. She glanced at him once or twice corroboratively, and said to herself that she had not been mistaken: he had real distinction—he was not of the herd. Then she picked up broad, crisp leaves with the point of her parasol and pondered while he talked of a possible walking tour in the Tyrol. Presently she broke in irrelevantly, hurriedly.

"I like to do a definite thing in a definite way: don't you?"

"Certainly; yes, of course."

"Well; and that is why I waited till this afternoon to tell you—to tell you——"

"To tell me——"

"My dear Mr. Ancram, that I cannot possibly marry you."

She had intended to put it differently, more effectively—perhaps with a turn that would punish him for his part in making the situation what it was. But it seemed a more momentous thing than she thought, now that she came to do it; she had a sense that destiny was too heavy a thing to play with.

He gave her an official look, the look which refuses to allow itself to be surprised, and said "Really?" in a manner which expressed absolutely nothing except that she had his attention.

"I do not pretend," she went on, impaling her vanity upon her candour, "that this will give you the slightest pain. I have been quite conscious of the relation between us" (here she blushed) "for a very long time; and I am afraid you must understand that I have reached this decision without any undue distress—*moi aussi*."

She had almost immediately regained her note; she was wholly mistress of what she said. For an instant Ancram fancied that the bamboos and the mahogany trees and the flaming hibiscus bushes were unreal, that he was walking into a panorama, and it seemed to him that his steps were uncertain. He was carrying his silk hat, and he set himself mechanically to smooth it round and round with his right hand as he listened.

When she paused he could find nothing better to say than "Really?" again; and he added, "You can't expect me to be pleased."

"Oh, but I do," she returned promptly. "You are, aren't you?"

It seemed a friendly reminder of his best interests. It brought the bamboos back to a vegetable growth, and steadied Ancram's nerves. He continued to smooth his hat; but he recovered himself sufficiently to join her, at a bound, in the standpoint from which she seemed inclined to discuss the matter without prejudice.

"Since we are to be quite candid with each other," he said, smiling, "I'm not sure."

"Your candour has—artistic qualities—which make it different from other people's. At all events, you will be to-morrow: to-morrow you will thank Heaven fasting."

He looked at her with some of the interest she used to inspire in him before his chains began to gall him.

"Prickly creature!" he said. "Are *you* quite sure? Is your determination unalterable?"

"I acknowledge your politeness in asking me," she returned. "It is."

"Then I suppose I must accept it." He spoke slowly. "But for the *soulagement* you suggest I am afraid I must wait longer than to-morrow."

They walked on in silence, reached the rank edge of the pond, and turned to go back. The afternooon still hung mellow in mid air, and something of its tranquillity seemed to have descended between them. In their joint escape from their mutual burden they experienced a reciprocal good feeling, something like comradeship, not untouched by sentiment. Once or twice he referred to their broken bond, asking her, with the appetite of his egotism, to give him the crystal truth of the reason she had accepted him.

"I accepted my idea of you," she said simply, "which was not altogether an accurate one. Besides, I think a good deal about—a lot of questions of administration. I thought I would like to have a closer interest, perhaps a hand in them. Such fools of women do."

After which they talked in a friendly way (it has been noted that Ancram was tolerant) about how essential ambition was to the bearableness of life in India.

"I see that you will be a much more desirable acquaintance," Rhoda said once, brightly, "now that I am not going to marry you." And he smiled in somewhat unsatisfied acquiescence.

Ancram grew silent as they drew near the main avenue and the real parting. The dusk had fallen suddenly, and a little wind brought showers of yellow leaves out of the shivering bamboos. They were quite alone, and at a short distance almost indistinguishable from the ixora bushes and the palmettos.

"Rhoda," he said, stopping short, "this is our last walk together—we who were to have walked together always. May I kiss you?"

The girl hesitated for an instant. "No," she said, with a nervous laugh: "not that. It would be like the resurrection of something that had never lived and never died!"

But she gave him her hand, and he kissed that, with some difficulty in determining whether he was grateful or aggrieved.

"It's really very raw," said Miss Daye, as they approached the others; "don't you think you had better put on your hat?"

CHAPTER XI.

"RHODA," said Mrs. Daye, as her daughter entered the drawing-room next morning, "I have thought it all out, and have decided to ask them. Mrs. St. George quite agrees with me. *She* says, sound the Military Secretary first, and of course I will; but she thinks they are certain to accept. Afterward we'll have the whole party photographed on the back verandah—I don't see how they could get out of it—and that will be a souvenir for you, if you like."

The girl sank into a deep easy chair and crossed her knees with deliberation. She was paler than usual; she could not deny a certain lassitude. As her mother spoke she put up her hand to hide an incipient yawn, and then turned her suffused eyes upon that lady, with the effect of granting a weary but necessary attention.

"You have decided to ask them?" she asked, with absent-minded interrogation. "Whom?"

"How ridiculous you are, Rhoda! The Viceroy and Lady Scansleigh, of course! As if there could be the slightest doubt about anybody else! You will want to know next what I intend to ask them to. I have never known a girl take so little interest in her own wedding."

"That brings us to the point," said Rhoda.

An aroused suspicion shot into Mrs. Daye's brown eyes. "What point, pray? No nonsense, now, Rhoda!"

"No nonsense this time, mummie; but no wedding either. I have decided—finally—not to marry Mr. Ancram."

Mrs. Daye sat upright—pretty, plump, determined. She really looked at the moment as if she could impose her ideas upon anybody. She had a perception of the effect, to this end, of an impressive *tournure*. Involuntarily she put a wispish curl in its place, and presented to her daughter the outline of an unexceptionable shoulder and sleeve.

"Your decision comes too late to be effectual, Rhoda. People do not change their minds in such matters when the wedding invitations are actually——"

"Written out to be lithographed—but not ordered yet, mummie."

"In half an hour they will be."

"Would have been, mummie dear."

Mrs. Daye assumed the utmost severity possible to a countenance intended to express only the amenities of life, and took her three steps toward the door. "This is childish, Rhoda," she said over her shoulder, "and I will not remain to listen to it. Retraction on your part at this hour would be nothing short of a crying scandal, and I assure you once for all that neither your father nor I will hear of it."

Mrs. Daye reached the door very successfully. Rhoda turned her head on its cushion, and looked after her mother in silence, with a half-deprecating smile. Having achieved the effect of her retreat, that lady turned irresolutely.

"I cannot remain to listen to it," she repeated, and stooped to pick up a pin.

"Oh, do remain, mummie! Don't behave like the haughty and hard-hearted mamma of primitive fiction; she is such an old-fashioned person. Do remain and be a nice, reasonable, up-to-date mummie: it will save such a lot of trouble."

"You don't seem to realise what you are talking of throwing over!"

Mrs. Daye, in an access of indignation, came as far back as the piano.

"Going down to dinner before the wives of the Small Cause Court! What a worldly lady it is!"

"I wish," Mrs. Daye ejaculated mentally, "that I had been brought up to manage daughters." What she said aloud, with the effect of being forced to do so, was that Rhoda had also apparently forgotten that her sister Lettice was to come out next year. Before the gravity of this proposition Mrs. Daye sank into the nearest chair. And the expense, with new frocks for Darjiling, would be really——

"All the arguments familiar to the pages of the *Family Herald*," the girl retorted, a dash of bitterness in her amusement, "'with a little store of maxims, preaching down a daughter's heart!' Aren't you ashamed, mummie! But you needn't worry about that. I'll go back to England and live with Aunt Jane: she dotes on me. Or I'll enter the Calcutta Medical College and qualify as a lady-doctor. I shouldn't like the cutting up, though—I really shouldn't."

"Rhoda, *tu me fais mal!* If you could only be serious for five minutes together. I suppose you have some absurd idea that Mr. Ancram is not sufficiently—demonstrative. But that will all come in due time, dear."

The girl laughed so uncontrollably that Mrs. Daye suspected herself of an unconscious witticism, and reflected a compromising smile.

"You think I could win his affections afterwards. Oh! I should despair of it. You have no idea how coy he is, mummie!"

Mrs. Daye made a little grimace of sympathy, and threw up her eyes and her hands. They laughed together, and then the elder lady said with severity that her daughter was positively indecorous. "Nothing could have been more devoted than his conduct yesterday afternoon. 'How ridiculously happy,' was what Mrs. St. George said—'how ridiculously happy those two are!'"

Mrs. Daye had become argumentative and plaintive. She imparted the impression that if there was another point of view—which she doubted—she was willing to take it.

"Oh! no doubt it was evident enough," Rhoda said tranquilly: "we had both been let off a bad bargain. An afternoon I shall always remember with pleasure."

"Then you have actually done it—broken with him!"

"Yes."

"Irrevocably?"

"Very much so."

"*Do* tell me how he took it!"

"Calmly. With admirable fortitude. It occupied altogether about ten minutes, with digressions. I've never kept any of his notes—he doesn't write clever notes—and you know I've always refused to wear a ring. So there was nothing to return except Buzz, which wouldn't have been fair to Buzz. It won't make a scandal, will it, my keeping Buzz? He's quite a changed dog since I've had him, and I love him for himself alone. He doesn't look in the least," Rhoda added, thoughtfully regarding the terrier curled up on the sofa, who turned his brown eyes on her and wagged his tail without moving, "like a Secretariat puppy."

"And is that all?"

"That's all—practically."

"Well, Rhoda, of course I had to think of your interests first—*any* mother would; but if it's really quite settled, I must confess that I believe you are well out of it, and I'm rather relieved myself. When I thought of being that man's mother-in-law I used to be thankful sometimes that your father would retire so soon—which was horrid, dear."

"I can understand your feelings, mummie."

"I'm sure you can, dear: you are always my sympathetic child. *I* wouldn't have married him for worlds! I never could imagine how you made up your mind to it in the first place.

Now, I suppose that absurd Mrs. St. George will go on with her theory that no daughter of mine will ever marry in India, because the young men find poor old me so amusing!"

"She's a clever woman—Mrs. St. George," Rhoda observed.

"And now that we've had our little talk, dear, there's one thing I should like you to take back—that quotation from Longfellow, or was it Mrs. Hemans?—about a daughter's heart, you know." Mrs. Daye inclined her head coaxingly towards the side. "I *shouldn't* like to have that to remember between us, dear," she said, and blew her nose with as close an approach to sentiment as could possibly be achieved in connection with that organ.

"You ridiculous old mummie! I assure you it hadn't the slightest application."

"Then *that's* all right," Mrs. Daye returned, in quite her sprightly manner. "I'll refuse the St. Georges' dinner on Friday night; it's only decent that we should keep rather quiet for a fortnight or so, till it blows over a little. And we shall get rid of you, my dear child, I'm perfectly certain, quite soon enough," she added over her shoulder, as she rustled out. "With your brains, you might even marry very well at home. But your father is sure to be put out about this—awfully put out!"

"Do you know, Buzz," murmured Rhoda a moment later (the terrier had jumped into her lap), "if I had been left an orphan in my early youth, I fancy I would have borne it better than most people."

CHAPTER XII.

THE editor of the *Word of Truth* sat in his office correcting a proof. The proof looked insurmountably difficult of correction, because it was printed in Bengali; but Tarachand Mookerjee's eye ran over it nimbly, and was accompanied by a smile, ever expanding and contracting, of pleased, almost childish appreciation. The day was hot, unusually so for February; and as the European editors up-town worked in their shirt-sleeves, so Tarachand Mookerjee worked in his *dhoty*, which left him bare from his waist up—bare and brown and polished, like a figure carved in mahogany, for his ribs were very visible. He wore nothing else, except patent leather shoes and a pair of white cotton stockings, originally designed for a more muscular limb, if for a weaker sex. These draperies were confined below the knee by pieces of the red tape with which a considerate Government tied up the reports and resolutions it sent the editor of the *Word of Truth* for review. Above Tarachand's three-cornered face his crisp black hair stood in clumps of oily and admired disorder; he had early acquired the literary habit of running his fingers through it. He had gentle, velvety eyes, and delicate features, and a straggling beard. He had lost two front teeth, and his attenuated throat was well sunk between his narrow shoulders. This gave him the look of a poor nervous creature; and, indeed, there was not a black-and-white terrier in Calcutta that could not have frightened him horribly. Yet he was not in the least afraid of a watch-dog belonging to Government—an official translator who weekly rendered up a confidential report of the emanations of the *Word of Truth* in English—because he knew that this animal's teeth were drawn by the good friends of Indian progress in the English Parliament.

Tarachand did almost everything that had to be done for the *Word of Truth* except the actual printing; although he had a nephew at the Scotch Mission College who occasionally wrote a theatrical notice for him in consideration of a free ticket, and who never ceased to urge him to print the paper in English, so that he, the nephew, might have an opportunity of practising composition in that language. It was Tarachand who translated the news out of the European papers into his own columns, where it read backwards, who reviewed the Bengali school-books written by the pundits of his acquaintance, who "fought" the case of the baboo in the Public Works Department dismissed for the trivial offence of stealing blotting-paper. It was, above all, Tarachand who wrote editorials about the conduct of the Government of India: that was the business of his life, his morning and his evening meditation. Tarachand had a great pull over the English editors uptown here; had a great pull, in fact, over any editors anywhere who felt compelled to base their opinions upon facts, or to express them with an eye upon consequences. Tarachand knew nothing about facts—it is doubtful whether he would recognise one if he saw it—and consequences did not exist for him. In place of these drawbacks he had the great advantages of imagination and invective. He was therefore able to write the most graphic editorials.

He believed them, too, with the open-minded, admiring simplicity that made him wax and wane in smiles over this particular proof. I doubt whether Tarachand could be brought to understand the first principles of veracity as applied to public affairs, unless possibly through his pocket. A definition to the Aryan mind is always best made in rupees, and to be mulcted heavily by a court of law might give him a grieved and surprised, but to some extent convincing education in political ethics. It would necessarily interfere at the same time, however, with his untrammelled and joyous talent for the creation and circulation of cheap fiction; it would be a hard lesson, and in the course of it Tarachand would petition with fervid loyalty and real tears. Perhaps it was on some of these accounts that the Government of India had never run Tarachand in.

Even for an editor's office it was a small room, and though it was on the second floor, the walls looked as if fungi grew on them in the rains. The floor was littered with publications; for the *Word of Truth* was taken seriously in Asia and in Oxford, and "exchanged" with a number of periodicals devoted to theosophical research, or the destruction of the opium revenue, or the protection of the sacred cow by combination against the beef-eating Briton. In one corner lay a sprawling blue heap of the reports and resolutions before mentioned, accumulating the dust of the year, at the end of which Tarachand would sell them for waste paper. For the rest, there was the editorial desk, with a chair on each side of it, the editorial gum-pot and scissors and waste-paper basket; and portraits, cut from the *Illustrated London News*, askew on the wall and wrinkling in their frames, of Max Müller and Lord Ripon. The warm air was heavy with the odour of fresh printed sheets, and sticky with Tarachand's personal anointing of cocoa-nut oil, and noisy with the clamping of the press below, the scolding of the crows, the eternal wrangle of the streets. Through the open window one saw the sunlight lying blindly on the yellow-and-pink upper stories, with their winding outer staircases and rickety balconies and narrow barred windows, of the court below.

Tarachand finished his proof and put it aside to cough. He was bent almost double, and still coughing when Mohendra Lal Chuckerbutty came in; so that the profusion of smiles with which he welcomed his brother journalist was not undimmed with tears. They embraced strenuously, however, and Mohendra, with a corner of his nether drapery, tenderly wiped the eyes of Tarachand. For the moment the atmosphere became doubly charged with oil and sentiment, breaking into a little storm of phrases of affection and gestures of respect. When it had been gone through with, these gentlemen of Bengal sat opposite each other beaming, and turned their conversation into English as became gentlemen of Bengal.

"I deplore," said Mohendra Lal Chuckerbutty concernedly, with one fat hand outspread on his knee, "to see that this iss still remaining with you——"

The other, with a gesture, brushed his ailment away. "Oh, it iss nothing—nothing whatever! I have been since three days under astronomical treatment of Dr. Chatterjee. 'Sir,' he remarked me yesterday, as I was leaving his höwwse, 'after *one* month you will be again salubrious. You will be on legs again—*take* my word!'"

Mohendra leaned back in his chair, put his head on one side, and described a right angle with one leg and the knee of the other. "Smart chap, Chatterjee!" he said, in perfect imitation of the casual sahib. He did not even forget to smooth his chin judicially as he said it. The editor of the *Word of Truth*, whose social opportunities had been limited to his own caste, looked on with admiration.

"And what news do you bring? But already I have perused the *Bengal Free Press* of to-day, so without doubt I know all the news!" Tarachand made this professional compliment as coyly and insinuatingly as if he and Mohendra had been sweethearts. "I can*not* withhold my congratulations on that leader of thiss morning," he went on fervently. "Here it is to my hand; diligently I have been studying it with awful admiration."

Mohendra's chin sank into his neck in a series of deprecating nods and inarticulate expressions of dissent, and his eyes glistened. Tarachand took up the paper and read from it :—

"'THE SATRAP AND THE COLLEGES.'

"Ah, how will His Honour look when he sees that!

"'Is it possible, we ask all sane men with a heart in their bosom, that Dame Rumour is right in her prognostications? Can it be true that the tyrant of Belvedere will dare to lay his hand on the revenue sacredly put aside to shower down upon our young hopefuls the mother's milk of an Alma Mater upon any pretext whatsoever? We fear the affirmative. Even as we go to press the knell of higher education may be sounding, and any day poor Bengal may learn from a rude Notification in the *Gazette* that her hope of progress has been shattered by the blasting pen of the caitiff Church. We will not mince matters, nor hesitate to proclaim to the housetops that the author of this dastardly action is but a poor stick. Doubtless he will say that the College grants are wanted for this or for that; but full well the people of this province know it is to swell the fat pay of boot-licking English officials that they are wanted. A wink is as good as a nod to a blind horse, and any excuse will serve when an autocrat without fear of God or man sits upon the *gaddi*. Many are the pitiable cases of hardship that will now come to view. One amongst thousands will serve. Known to the writer is a family man, and a large one. He has been blessed with seven sons, all below the age of nine. Up to the present he has been joyous as a lark and playful as a kitten, trusting in the goodness of Government to provide the nutrition of their minds and livelihoods. Now he is beating his breast, for his treasures will be worse than orphans. How true are the words of the poet—

> "'Manners with fortunes, humours turn with climes,
> Tenets with books, and principles with times!'

Again and yet again have we exposed the hollow, heartless and vicious policy of the acting Lieutenant-Governor, but, alas! without result.

> "'Destroy his fib or sophistry—in vain;
> The creature's at his dirty work again!'

But will this province sit tamely down under its brow-beating? A thousand times no! We will appeal to the justice, to the mercy of England, through our noble friends in Parliament, and the lash will yet fall like a scorpion upon the shrinking hide of the coward who would filch the people from their rights.'"

Tarachand stopped to cough, and his round liquid eyeballs, as he turned them upon Mohendra, stood out of their creamy whites with enthusiasm. "One word," he cried, as soon as he had breath: "you are the Macaulay of Bengal! No less. The Macaulay of Bengal!"

(John Church, when he read Mohendra's article next day, laughed, but uneasily. He knew that in all Bengal there is no such thing as a sense of humour.)

"My own feeble pen," Tarachand went on deprecatingly, "has been busy at this thing for the to-morrow's issue. I also have been saying some worthless remark, perhaps not altogether beyond the point," and the corrected proof went across the table to Mohendra. While he glanced through it Tarachand watched him eagerly, reflecting every shade of expression that passed over the other man's face. When Mohendra smiled Tarachand laughed out with delight, when Mohendra looked grave Tarachand's countenance was sunk in melancholy.

"' Have the hearts of the people of India turned to water that any son of English mud may ride over their prostrate forms?'"

he read aloud in Bengali. "That is well said.

"' Too often the leaders of the people have waited on the Lieutenant-Governor to explain desirable matters, but the counsel of grey hairs has not been respected. Three Vedas, and the fourth a cudgel! The descendants of monkeys have forgotten that once before they played too many tricks. The white dogs want another lesson.'

"A-ha!" Mohendra paused to comment, smiling. "Very good talk. But it is necessary also to be a little careful. After that—it is my advice—you say how Bengalis are loyal before everything."

The editor of the *Word of Truth* slowly shook his head, showing, in his contemptuous amusement, a row of glittering teeth stained with the red of the betel. "No harm can come," he said. "They dare not muzzle thee press."

The phrase was pat and familiar. "When the loin-cloth burns one must speak out. I am a poor man, and I have sons. Where is their rice to come from? Am I a man without shame, that I should let the Sirkar turn them into carpenters?" In his excitement Tarachand had dropped into his own tongue.

"'Education to Bengalis is as dear as religion. They have fought for religion, they may well fight for education. Let the game go on; let European officials grow fat on our taxes; let the wantons, their women, dance in the arms of men, and look into their faces with impudence, at the *tamashos* of the Burra Lât as before. But if the Sirkar robs the poor Bengali of his education let him beware. He will become without wings or feathers, while Shiva will protect the helpless and those with a just complaint.'

"Without doubt that will make a *sen*sation," Mohendra said, handing back the proof. "Without doubt! You can have much more the courage of your opinion in the vernacular. English—that iss a*noth*er thing. I wrote mysé-êlf, last week, some issmall criticism on the

Chairman of the Municipality, maybe half a column—about that new drain in Colootollah which we must put our hand in our pocket. Yesterda-ay I met the Chairman on the Red Road, and he takes no notiss off my face! That was *not* pleasant. To-day I am writing on issecond thoughts we cannot live without drainage, and I will send him marked copy. But in that way it iss troublesome, the English."

"These Europeans they have no eye-shame. They are entirely made of wood. But I think this Notification will be a nice kettle of fish! Has the Committee got isspeakers for the mass meeting on the Maidan?"

Mohendra nodded complacently. "Already it is being arranged. For a month I have known every word spoken by His Honour on this thing. I have the *best* information. Every week I am watching the *Gazette*. The morning of publication *ekdum*[*] goes telegram to our good friend in Parliament. Agitation in England, agitation in India! Either will come another Royal Com-

---

[*] In one breath.

mission to upset the thing, or the Lieutenant-Governor is forced to *re*tire."

Mohendra's nods became oracular. Then his expression grew seriously regretful. "Mysé-êlf I hope they will—what iss it in English?—*w'itewass* him with a commission. It goes against me to see disgrace on a high official. It is *not* pleasant. He means well—he *means* well. And at heart he is a very good fellow—personally I have had much agreeable conversation with him. Always he has asked me to his garden-parties."

"He has set fire to his own beard, brother," said the editor of the *Word of Truth* in the vernacular, spitting.

"Very true—oh, very true! And all the more we must attack him because I see the reptile English press, in Calcutta, in Bombay, in Allahabad, they are upholding this dacoity. That iss the only word—dacoity." Mohendra rose. "And we two have both off us the best occasion to fight," he added beamingly, as he took his departure, "for did we not graduate hand in hand that same year out off Calcutta University?"

．　　．　　．　　．　　．　　．　　．

"God knows, Ancram, I believe it is the right thing to do!"

John Church had reached his difficult moment—the moment he had learned to dread. It lay in wait for him always at the end of unbaffled investigation, of hard-fast steering by principle, of determined preliminary action of every kind—the actual executive moment. Neither the impulse of his enthusiasm nor the force of his energy ever sufficed to carry him over it comfortably; rather, at this point, they ebbed back, leaving him stranded upon his responsibility, which invariably at once assumed the character of a quicksand. He was never defeated by himself at these junctures, but he hated them. He turned out from himself then, consciously seeking support and reinforcement, to which at other times he was indifferent; and it was in a crisis of desire for encouragement that he permitted himself to say to Lewis Ancram that God knew he believed the College Grants Notification was the right thing to do. He had asked Ancram to wait after the Council meeting was over very much for this purpose.

"Yes, sir," the Chief Secretary replied; "if I may be permitted to say so, it is the most conscientious piece of legislation of recent years."

The Lieutenant-Governor looked anxiously at Ancram from under his bushy eyebrows, and then back again at the Notification. It lay in broad margined paragraphs of beautiful round baboo's handwriting, covering a dozen pages of foolscap, before him on the table. It waited only for his ultimate decision to go to the Government Printing Office and appear in the *Gazette* and be law to Bengal. Already he had approved each separate paragraph. His Chief Secretary had never turned out a better piece of work.

"To say precisely what is in my mind, Ancram," Church returned, beginning to pace the empty chamber, "I have sometimes thought that you were not wholly with me in this matter."

"I will not disguise from you, sir"—Ancram spoke with candid emphasis—"that I think it's a risky thing to do, a—deuced risky thing." His Honour was known to dislike strong language.

"But as to the principle involved there can be no two opinions."

His Honour's gaunt shadow passed and repassed against the oblong patch of westering February sunlight that lightened the opposite wall before he replied.

"I am prepared for an outcry," he said slowly at last. "I think I can honestly say that I am concerned only with the principle—with the possible harm, and the probable good."

Ancram felt a rising irritation. He reflected that if His Honour had chosen to take him into confidence earlier, he—Mr. Ancram—might have been saved a considerable amount of moral unpleasantness. By taking him into confidence now the Lieutenant-Governor merely added to it appreciably and, Ancram pointed out to himself, undeservedly. He played with his watch-chain for distraction, and looked speculatively at the Notification, and said that one thing was certain, they could depend upon His Excellency if it came to any nonsense with the Secretary of State. "Scansleigh is loyal to his very marrow. He'll stand by us, whatever happens." No one admired the distinguishing characteristic of the Viceroy of India more than the Chief Secretary of the Government of Bengal.

"Scansleigh sees it as I do," Church returned; "and I see it plainly. At least I have not spared myself—nor any one else," he added, with a smile of admission which was at the moment pathetic, "in working the thing up. My action has no bearing that I have not carefully examined. Nothing can result from it that I do not expect—at least approximately—to happen."

Ancram almost imperceptibly raised his eyebrows. The gesture, with its suggestion of dramatic superiority, was irresistible to him; he would have made it if Church had been looking at him; but the eyes of the Lieutenant-Governor were fixed upon the sauntering multitude in the street below. He turned from the window, and went on with a kind of passion.

"I tell you, Ancram, I feel my responsibility in this thing, and I will not carry it any longer in the shape of a curse to my country. I don't speak of the irretrievable mischief that is being done by the wholesale creation of a clerkly class for whom there is no work, or of the danger of putting that sharpest tool of modern progress—higher education—into hands that can only use it to destroy. When we have helped these people to shatter all their old notions of reverence and submission and self-abnegation and piety, and given them, for such ideals as their fathers had, the scepticism and materialism of the West, I don't know that we shall have accomplished much to our credit. But let that pass. The ultimate consideration is this: You know and I know where the money comes from—the three lakhs and seventy-five thousand rupees—that goes every year to make B.A.s of Calcutta University. It's a commonplace to say that it is sweated in annas and pice out of the cultivators of the villages—poor devils who live and breed and rot in pest-stricken holes we can't afford to drain for them, who wear one rag the year through and die of famine when the rice harvest fails! The ryot pays, that the money-lender who screws him and the landowner who bullies him may give their sons a cheap European education."

"The wonder is," Ancram replied, "that it has not been acknowledged a beastly shame long ago. The vested interest has never been very strong."

"Ah well," Church said more cheerfully, " we have provided for the vested interest; and my technical schools will, I hope, go some little way toward providing for the cultivators. At all events they will teach him to get more out of his fields. It's a tremendous problem, that," he added, refolding the pages with a last glance, and slipping them into their cover: "the ratio at which population is increasing out here and the limited resources of the soil."

He had reassumed the slightly pedantic manner that was characteristic of him; he was again dependent upon himself, and resolved.

"Send it off at once, will you?" he said; and Ancram gave the packet to a waiting messenger. "A weighty business off my mind," he added, with a sigh of relief. "Upon my word, Ancram, I am surprised to find you so completely in accord with me. I fancied you would have objections to make at the last moment, and that I should have to convince you. I rather wanted to convince somebody. But I am very pleased indeed to be disappointed!"

"It is a piece of work which has my sincerest admiration, sir," Ancram answered; and as the two men descended the staircases from the Bengal Council Chamber to the street, the Lieutenant-Governor's hand rested upon the arm of his Chief Secretary in a way that was almost affectionate.

CHAPTER XIII.

THREE days later the Notification appeared. John Church sat tensely through the morning, unconsciously preparing himself for emergencies —deputations, petitions, mobs. None of these occurred. The day wore itself out in the usual routine, and in the evening His Honour was somewhat surprised to meet at dinner a member of the Viceroy's Council who was not aware that anything had been done. He turned with some eagerness next morning to the fourth page of his newspaper, and found its leading article illuminating the subject of an archæological discovery in Orissa, made some nine months previously. The Lieutenant-Governor was an energetic person, and did not understand the temper of Bengal. He had published a Notification subversive of the educational policy of the Government for sixty years, and he expected this proceeding to excite immediate attention. He gave it an importance almost equal to that of the Derby Sweepstakes. This, however, was in some degree excusable, considering the short time he had spent in Calcutta and the persevering neglect he had shown in observing the tone of society.

Even the telegram to the sympathetic Member of Parliament failed of immediate transmission. Mohendra Lal Chuckerbutty wrote it out with emotion; then he paused, remembering that the cost of telegrams paid for by enthusiastic private persons was not easily recoverable from committees. Mohendra was a solid man, but there were funds for this purpose. He decided that he was not justified in speeding the nation's cry for succour at his own expense; so he submitted the telegram to the committee, which met at the end of the week. The committee asked Mohendra to cut it down and let them see it again. In the end it arrived at Westminster almost as soon as the mail. Mohendra, besides, had his hands and his paper full, at the moment, with an impassioned attack upon an impulsive judge of the High Court who had shot a bullock with its back broken. As to the *Word of Truth*, Tarachand Mookerjee was celebrating his daughter's wedding, at the time the Notification was published, with tom-toms and sweetmeats and a very expensive nautch, and for three days the paper did not appear at all.

The week lengthened out, and the Lieutenant-Governor's anxiety grew palpably less. His confidence had returned to such a degree that when the officers of the Education Department absented themselves in a body from the first of his succeeding entertainments he was seriously disturbed. "It's childish," he said to Judith. "By my arrangement not a professor among them will lose a pice either in pay or pension. If the people are anxious enough for higher education to pay twice as much for it as they do now these fellows will go on with their lectures. If not, we'll turn them into inspectors, or superintendents of the technical schools."

"I can understand a certain soreness on the subject of their dignity," his wife suggested.

Church frowned impatiently. "People might think less of their dignity in this country and more of their duty, with advantage," he said, and she understood that the discussion was closed.

The delay irritated Ancram, who was a man of action. He told other people that he feared it was only the ominous lull before the storm, and assured himself that no man could hurry Bengal. Nevertheless, the terms in which he advised Mohendra Lal Chuckerbutty, who came to see him every Sunday afternoon, were successful to the point of making that Aryan drive rather faster on his way back to the *Bengal Free Press* office. At the end of a fortnight Mr. Ancram was able to point to the verification of his prophecy; it had been the lull before the storm, which developed, two days later, in the columns of the native press, into a tornado.

"I tell you," said he, "you might as well petition Sri Krishna as the Viceroy," when Mohendra Lal Chuckerbutty reverted to this method of obtaining redress. Mohendra, who was a Hindoo of orthodoxy, may well have found this flippant, but he only smiled, and assented, and went away and signed the petition. He yielded to the natural necessity of the pathetic temperament of his countrymen—even when they were university graduates and political agitators—to implore before they did anything else. An appeal was distilled and forwarded. The Viceroy promptly indicated the nature of his opinions by refusing to receive this document unless it reached him through the proper channel—which was the Bengal Government. The prayer of humility then became a shriek of defiance, a transition accomplished with remarkable rapidity in Bengal. In one night Calcutta flowered mysteriously into coloured cartoons, depicting the Lieutenant-Governor in the prisoner's dock, charged by the Secretary of State, on the bench, with the theft of bags of gold marked "College Grants"; while the Director of Education, weeping bitterly, gave evidence against him. The Lieutenant-Governor was represented in a green frock-coat and the Secretary of State in a coronet, which made society laugh, and started a wave of interest in the College Grants Notification. John Church saw it in people's faces at his garden parties, and it added to the discomfort with which he read advertisements of various mass meetings, in protest, to be held throughout the province, and noticed among the speakers invariably the unaccustomed names of the Rev. Professor Porter of the Exeter Hall Institute, the Rev. Dr. MacInnes of the Caledonian Mission, and Father Ambrose, who ruled St. Dominic's College, and who certainly insisted, as part of *his* curriculum, upon the lives of the Saints.

The afternoon of the first mass meeting in Calcutta closed into the evening of the last ball of the season at Government House. A petty royalty from Southern Europe, doing the grand tour, had trailed his clouds of glory rather indolently late into Calcutta; and, as society anxiously emphasized, there was practically only a single date available before Lent for a dance in his honour. When it was understood that Their Excellencies would avail themselves of this somewhat contracted opportunity, society beamed upon itself, and said it knew they would—they were the essence of hospitality.

There are three square miles of the green Maidan, round which Calcutta sits in a stucco semi-circle, and past which her brown river runs to the sea. Fifteen thousand people, therefore, gathered in one corner of it, made a somewhat unusually large patch of white upon the grass, but were not otherwise impressive, and in no wise threatening. Society, which had forgotten about the mass meeting, put up its eye-glass, driving on the Red Road, and said that there was evidently something "going on"— probably a football team of Tommies from the Fort playing the town. Only two or three elderly officials, taking the evening freshness in solitary walks, looked with anxious irritation at the densely-packed mass; and Judith Church, driving home through the smoky yellow twilight, understood the meaning of the cheers the south wind softened and scattered abroad. They brought her a stricture of the heart with the thought of John Church's devotion to these people. Ingrates, she named them to herself, with compressed lips—ingrates, traitors, hounds! Her eyes filled with the impotent tears of a woman's pitiful indignation; her heart throbbed with a pang of new recognition of her husband's worth, and of tenderness for it, and of unrecognised pain beneath that even this could not constitute him her hero and master. She asked herself bitterly—I fear her politics were not progressive—what the people in England meant by encouraging open and ignorant sedition in India, and whole passages came eloquently into her mind of the speech she would make in Parliament if she were but a man and a member. They brought her some comfort, but she dismissed them presently to reflect seriously whether something might not be done. She looked courageously at the possibility of imprisoning Dr. MacInnes. Then she too thought of the ball, and subsided upon the determination of consulting Lewis Ancram, at the ball, upon this point. She drew a distinct ethical satisfaction from her intention. It seemed in the nature of a justification for the quickly pulsating pleasure with which she looked forward to the evening.

CHAPTER XIV.

GENTLEMEN native to Bengal are not usually invited to balls at Government House. It is unnecessary to speak of the ladies: they are non-existent to the social eye, even if it belongs to a Viceroy. The reason is popularly supposed to be the inability of gentlemen native to Bengal to understand the waltz, except by Aryan analysis. It is thought well to circumscribe their opportunities of explaining it thus, and they are asked instead to evening parties which offer nothing more stimulating to the imagination than conversation and champagne—of neither of which they partake. On this occasion, however, at the entreaty of the visiting royalty, the rule was relaxed to admit perhaps fifty; and when Lewis Ancram arrived—rather late—the first personality he recognised as in any way significant was that of Mohendra Lal Chuckerbutty, who leaned against a pillar, with his hands clasped behind him, raptly contemplating a polka. Mohendra, too, had an appreciation of personalities, and of his respectful duty to them. He bore down in Ancram's direction unswervingly through the throng, his eye humid with happiness, his hand held out in an impulse of affection. When he thought he had arrived at the Chief Secretary's elbow he looked about him in some astonishment. A couple of subalterns in red jackets disputed with mock violence over the dance-card of a little girl in white, and a much larger lady was waiting with imposing patience until he should be pleased to get off her train. At the same moment an extremely correct black back glanced through the palms into the verandah.

The verandah was very broad and high, and softly lighted in a way that made vague glooms visible and yet gave a gentle radiance to the sweep of pale-tinted drapery that here and there suggested a lady sunk in the depths of a roomy arm-chair, playing with her fan and talking in undertones. It was a place of delicious mystery, in spite of the strains of the orchestra that throbbed out from the ball-room, in spite of the secluded fans opening and closing in some commonplace of Calcutta flirtation. The mystery came in from without, where the stars crowded down thick and luminous behind the palms, and a grey mist hung low in the garden beneath, turning it into a fantasy of shadowed forms and filmy backgrounds and new significances. Out there, in the wide spaces beyond the tall verandah pillars, the spirit of the spring was abroad —the troubled, throbbing, solicitous Indian spring, perfumed and tender. The air was warm and sweet and clinging; it made life a pathetic, enjoyable necessity, and love a luxury of much refinement.

Ancram folded his arms and stood in the doorway and permitted himself to feel these things. If he was not actually looking for Judith Church, it was because he was always, so to speak, anticipating her; in a state of readiness to receive the impression of her face, the music of her voice. Mrs. Church was the reason of the occasion, the reason of every occasion in so far as it concerned him. She seemed simply the corollary of his perception of the exquisite night when he discovered her presently, on one of the more conspicuous sofas, talking to Sir Peter Bloomsbury. She was waiting for him to find her, with a little flickering smile that came in the pauses between Sir Peter's remarks; and when Ancram approached he noticed, with as keen a pleasure as he was capable of feeling, that her replies to this dignitary were made somewhat at random.

Their conversation changed when Sir Peter went away only to take its note of intimacy and its privilege of pauses. They continued to speak of trivial matters, and to talk in tones and in things they left unsaid. His eyes lingered in the soft depths of hers to ascertain whether the roses were doing well this year at Belvedere, and there was a conscious happiness in the words with which she told him that they were quite beyond her expectations not wholly explicable even by so idyllic a fact. The content of their neigbourhood surrounded them like an atmosphere, beyond which people moved about irrationally and a string band played unmeaning selections much too loud. She was lovelier than he had ever seen her, more his possession than he had ever felt her—the incarnation, as she bent her graceful head towards him, of the eloquent tropical night and the dreaming tropical spring. He told himself afterwards that he felt at this moment an actual pang of longing, and rejoiced that he could still experience an undergraduate's sensation after so many years of pleasures that were but aridly intellectual at their best. Certainly, as he sat there in his irreproachable clothes and attitude, he knew that his blood was beating warm to his finger-tips with a delicious impulse to force the sweet secret of the situation between them. The south wind suggested to him, through the scent of breaking buds, that prudence was entirely a relative thing, and not even relative to a night like this and a woman like that. As he looked at a tendril of her hair, blown against the warm whiteness of her neck, it occurred to the Honourable Mr. Ancram that he might go a little further. He felt divinely rash; but his intention was to go only a little further. Hitherto he had gone no distance at all.

The south wind drove them along together. Judith felt it on her neck and arms, and in little, cool, soft touches about her face. She did not pause to question the happiness it brought her: there were other times for pauses and questions; her eyes were ringed with them, under the powder. She abandoned herself to her woman's divine sense of ministry; and the man she loved observed that she did it with a certain inimitable poise, born of her confidence in him, which was as new as it was entrancing.

People began to flock downstairs to supper in the wake of the Viceroy and the visiting royalty; the verandah emptied itself. Presently they became aware that they were alone.

"You have dropped your fan," Ancram said, and picked it up. He looked at its device for a moment, and then restored it. Judith's hands were lying in her lap, and he slipped the fan into one of them, letting his own rest for a perceptible instant in the warm palm of the other. There ensued a tumultuous silence. He had only underscored a glance of hers; yet it seemed that he had created something—something as formidable as lovely, a embarrassing as divine. As he gently withdrew his hand she lifted her eyes to his with mute entreaty, and he saw that they were full of tears. He told himself afterwards that he had been profoundly moved; but this did not interfere with his realisation that it was an exquisite moment.

Ancram regarded her gravely, with a smile of much consideration. He gave her a moment of time, and then, as she did not look up again, he leaned forward, and said, quite naturally and evenly, as if the proposition were entirely legitimate: "The relation between us is too tacit. Tell me that you love me, dear."

For an instant he repented, since it seemed that she would be carried along on the sweet tide of his words to the brink of an indiscretion. Once more she looked up, softly seeking his eyes; and in hers he saw so lovely a light of self-surrender that he involuntarily thanked Heaven that there was no one else to recognise it. In her face was nothing but the thought of him; and, seeing this, he had a swift desire to take her in his arms and experience at its fullest and sweetest the sense that she and her little empire were gladly lost there. In the pause of her mute confession he felt the strongest exultation he had known. Her glance reached him like a cry from an unexplored country; the revelation of her love filled him with the knowledge that she was infinitely more adorable and more desirable than he had thought her. From that moment she realised to him a supreme good, and he never afterwards thought of his other ambitions without a smile of contempt which was almost genuine. But she said nothing: she seemed removed from any necessity of speech, lifted up on a wave of absolute joy, and isolated from all that lay either behind or before. He controlled his impatience for words from her—for he was very sure of one thing; that when they came they would be kind—and chose his own with taste.

"Don't you think that it would be better if we had the courage and the candour to accept things as they are? Don't you think we would be stronger for all that we must face if we acknowledged—only to each other—the pain and the sweetness of it?"

"I have never been blind," she said softly.

"All I ask is that you will not even pretend to be. Is that too much?"

"How can it be a question of that?" Her voice trembled a little. Then she hurried illogically on: "But there can be no change—there must be no change. These are things I hoped you would never say."

"The alternative is too wretched: to go on living a lie—and a stupid, unnecessary lie. Why, in Heaven's name, should there be the figment of hypocrisy between us? I know that I must be content with very little, but I am afraid there is no way of telling you how much I want that little."

She had grown very pale, and she put up her hand and smoothed her hair with a helpless, mechanical gesture.

"No, no," she said—"stop. Let us make an end of it quickly. I was very well content to go on with the lie. I think I should always have been content. But now there is no lie: there is nothing to stand upon any longer. You must get leave, or something, and go away—or I will. I am not—really—very well."

She looked at him miserably, with twitching lips, and he laid a soothing hand—there was still no one to see—upon her arm.

"Judith, don't talk of impossibilities. How could we two live in one world—and apart! Those are the heroics of a dear little schoolgirl. You and I are older, and braver."

She put his hand away with a touch that was a caress, but only said irrelevantly, "And Rhoda Daye might have loved you honestly!"

"Ah, that threadbare old story!" He felt as if she had struck him, and the feeling impelled him to ask her why she thought he deserved punishment. "Not that it hurts," Mr. Ancram added, almost resentfully.

She gave him a look of vague surprise, and then lapsed, refusing to make the effort to understand, into the troubled depths of her own thought.

"Be a little kind, Judith. I only want a word."

The south wind brought them a sound out of the darkness—the high, faint, long-drawn sound of a cheer from the Maidan. She lifted her head and listened intently, with apprehensive eyes. Then she rose unsteadily from her seat, and, as he gave her his arm in silence, she stood for a moment gathering up her strength, and waiting, it seemed, for the sound to come again. Nothing reached them but the wilder, nearer wail of the jackals in the streets.

"I must go home," she said, in a voice that was quite steady; "I must find my husband and go home."

He would have held her back, but she walked resolutely, if somewhat purposelessly, round the long curve of the verandah, and stood still, looking at the light that streamed out of the ball-room and glistened on the leaves of a range of palms and crotons in pots that made a seclusion there.

"Then," said Ancram, "I am to go on with the forlorn comfort of a guess. I ought to be thankful, I suppose, that you can't take that from me. Perhaps you would," he added bitterly, "if you could know how precious it is."

His words seemed to fix her in a half-formed resolve. Her hand slipped out of his arm, and she took a step away from him toward the crotons. Against their dark green leaves he saw, with some alarm, how white her face was.

"Listen," she said: "I think you do not realise it, but I know you are hard and cruel. You ask me if I am not to you what I ought to be to my husband, who is a good man, and who loves me, and trusts you. And, what is worse, this has come up between us at a time when he is threatened and troubled: on the very night when I meant—when I meant"—she stopped to conquer the sob in her throat—" to have asked you to think of something that might be done to help him. Well, but you ask me if I have come to love you, and perhaps in a way you have a right to know; and the truth is better, as you say. And I answer you that I have. I answer you yes, it is true, and I know it will always be true. But from to-night you will remember that every time I look into your face and touch your hand I hurt my own honour and my husband's, and—and you will not let me see you often."

As Ancram opened his lips to speak, the cheer from the Maidan smote the air again, and this time it seemed nearer. Judith took his arm nervously.

"What can they be doing out there?" she exclaimed. "Let us go—I must find my husband—let us go!"

They crossed the threshold into the ballroom, where John Church joined them almost immediately, his black brows lightened by an unusually cheerful expression.

"I've been having a long talk with His Excellency," he said to them jointly. "An uncommonly capable fellow, Scansleigh. He tells me he has written a strong private letter to the Secretary of State about this Notification of mine. That's bound to have weight, you know, in case they make an attempt to get hold of Parliament at home."

As Mrs. Church and Mr. Lewis Ancram left

the verandah a chair was suddenly pushed back behind the crotons. Miss Rhoda Daye had been sitting in the chair, alone too, with the south wind and the stars. She had no warning of what she was about to overhear—no sound had reached her, either of their talk or their approach—and in a somewhat agitated colloquy with herself she decided that nothing could be so terrible as her personal interruption of what Mrs. Church was saying. That lady's words, though low and rapid, were very distinct, and Rhoda heard them out involuntarily, with a strong disposition to applaud her and to love her. Then she turned a key upon her emotions and Judith Church's secret, and slipped quietly out to look for her mother, who asked her, between her acceptance of an ice from the Home Secretary and a *petit four* from the General Commanding the Division, why on earth she looked so depressed.

Ancram, turning away from the Churches, almost ran into the arms of Mohendra Lal Chuckerbutty, with whom he shook hands. His manner expressed, combined with all the

"What do I know about the speech!"

good will in the world, a slight embarrassment that he could not remember Mohendra's name, which is so often to be noticed when European officials have occasion to greet natives of distinction—natives of distinction are so very numerous and so very similar.

"I hope you are well!" beamed the editor of the *Bengal Free Press*. "It is a very select party." Then Mohendra dropped his voice confidentially: "We have sent to England, by to-day's mail, every word of the isspeech of Dr. MacInnes——"

"Damn you!" Ancram said, with a respectful, considering air: "what do I know about the speech of Dr. MacInnes! *Jehannum jao!*" *

Mohendra laughed in happy acquiescence as the Chief Secretary bowed and left him. "Certainlie! certainlie!" he said; "it is a very select party!"

The evening had one more incident. Mr. and Mrs. Church made their retreat early: Judith's

---

* "Go to Hades!"

face offered an excuse of fatigue which was better than her words. Their carriage turned out of Circular Road with a thickening crowd of natives talking noisily and walking in the same direction. They caught up with a glare and the smell and smoke of burning pitch. Judith said uneasily that there seemed to be a bonfire in the middle of the road. They drew a little nearer, and the crowd massed around them before and behind, on the bridge leading to Belvedere out of the city. Then John Church perceived that the light streamed from a burning figure which flamed and danced grotesquely, wired to a pole attached to a bullock cart and pulled along by coolies. The absorbed crowd that walked behind, watching and enjoying like excited children at a show, chattered defective English, and the light from the burning thing on the pole streamed upon faces already to some extent illumined by the higher culture of the University Colleges. But it was not until they recognised his carriage and outriders, and tried to hurry and to scatter on the narrow bridge, that the Acting Lieutenant-Governor of Bengal fully realised that he had been for some distance swelling a procession which was entertaining itself with much gusto at the expense of his own effigy.

CHAPTER XV.

WHEN it became obvious that the College Grants Notification held fateful possibilities for John Church personally, and for his wife incidentally, it rapidly developed into a topic. Ladies, in the course of midday visits in each other's cool drawing-rooms, repeated things their husbands had let fall at dinner the night before, and said they were awfully sorry for Mrs. Church; it must be too trying for her, poor thing. If it were only on *her* account, some of them thought, the Lieutenant-Governor—the "L.G.," they called him—ought to let things go on as they always had. What difference did it make anyway! At the clubs the matter superseded, for the moment, the case of an army chaplain accused of improper conduct at Singapore, and bets were freely laid on the issue—three to one that Church would be "smashed."

If this attitude seemed less sympathetic than that of the ladies, it betokened at least no hostility. On the contrary, no small degree of appreciation was current for His Honour. He would not have heard the matter discussed often from his own point of view, but that was because his own point of view was very much his own property. He might have heard himself commended from a good many others, however, and especially on the ground of his pluck. Men said between their cigars that very few fellows would care to put their hands to such a piece of *zubberdusti** at this end of the century, however much it was wanted. Personally they hoped the beggar would get it through, and with equal solicitude they proceeded to bet that he wouldn't. Among the sentiments the beggar evoked, perhaps the liveliest was one of gratitude for so undeniable a sensation so near the end of the cold weather, when sensations were apt to take flight, with other agreeable things, to the hill stations.

---

* " High-handed proceeding."

The storm reached a point when the Bishop felt compelled to put forth an allaying hand from the pulpit of the Cathedral. As the head of the Indian Establishment the Bishop felt himself allied in no common way with the governing power, and His Lordship was known to hold strong views on the propriety with which lawn sleeves might wave above questions of public importance. Besides, neither Dr. MacInnes nor Professor Porter were lecturing on the binomial theorem under Established guidance, while as to Father Ambrose, he positively invited criticism, with his lives of the Saints. When, therefore, the Cathedral congregation heard his Lordship begin his sermon with the sonorous announcement from Ecclesiastes,

"*For in much wisdom is much grief: and he that increaseth knowledge increaseth sorrow. He— that increaseth—knowledge—increaseth—sorrow,*"

it listened, with awakened interest, for a snub to Dr. MacInnes and Professor Porter, and for a rebuke, full of dignity and austerity, to Father

Ambrose; both of which were duly administered. His Lordship's views, supported by the original Preacher, were doubtless more valuable in his sermon than they would be here, but it is due to him to say that they formed the happiest combination of fealty and doctrine. The Honourable Mr. Ancram said to Sir William Scott on the Cathedral steps after the service— it was like the exit of a London theatre, with people waiting for their carriages—that while his Lordship's reference was very proper and could hardly fail to be of use, public matters looked serious when they came to be discussed in the pulpit. To which Sir William gave a deprecating agreement.

Returning to his somewhat oppressively lonely quarters, Ancram felt the need of further conversation. The Bishop had stirred him to vigorous dissent, which his Lordship's advantage of situation made peculiarly irritating to so skilled an observer of weak points. He bethought himself that he might write to Philip Doyle. He remembered that Doyle had not answered the letter in which he had written of his changed domestic future, frankly asking for congratulation rather than for condolence; but without resentment, for why should a man trouble himself under Florentine skies with unnecessary Calcutta correspondents? He consulted only his own pleasure in writing again: Doyle was so readily appreciative, he would see the humour in the development of affairs with His Honour. It was almost a week since Mr. Ancram had observed at the ball, with acute annoyance, what an unreasonable effect the matter was having upon Judith Church, and he was again himself able to see the humour of it. He finally wrote with much facility a graphically descriptive letter, in which the Bishop came in as a mere picturesque detail at the end. He seemed to pick his way, as he turned the pages, out of an embarrassing moral quagmire; he was so obviously high and dry when he could fix the whole thing in a caricature of effective paragraphs. He wrote:—

"I don't mind telling you privately that I have no respect whatever for the scheme, and very little for the author of it. He reminds one of nothing so much as an elderly hen sitting, with the obstinacy of her kind, on eggs out of which it is easy to see no addled reform will ever step to crow. He is as blind as a bat to his own deficiencies. I doubt whether even his downfall will convince him that his proper sphere of usefulness in life was that of a Radical cobbler. He has a noble preference for the ideal of an impeccable Indian administrator, which he goes about contemplating, while his beard grows with the tale of his blunders. The end, however, cannot be far off. Bengal is howling for his retirement; and, notwithstanding a fulsome habit he has recently developed of hanging upon my neck for sympathy, I own to you that, if circumstances permitted, I would howl too."

Ancram's first letter had miscarried, a peon in the service of the Sirkar having abstracted the stamps; and Philip Doyle, when he received the second, was for the moment overwhelmed with inferences from his correspondent's silence regarding the marriage, which should have been imminent when he wrote. Doyle glanced rapidly through another Calcutta letter that arrived with Ancram's for possible news; but the brief sensation of Miss Daye's broken engagement had expired long before it was written, and it contained no reference to the affair. The theory of a postponement suggested itself irresistibly; and he spent an absorbed and motionless twenty minutes, sitting on the edge of his bed, while his pipe went out in his hand, looking fixedly at the floor of his room in the hotel, and engaged in constructing the tissue of circumstances which would make such a thing likely. If he did not grow consciously lighter-hearted with this occupation, at least he turned, at the end of it, to reperuse his letters, as if they had brought him good news. He read them both carefully again, and opened the newspaper that came with the second. It was a copy of the *Bengal Free Press*, and his friend of the High Court had called his special attention to its leading article, as the most caustic and effective attack upon the College Grants Notification which had yet appeared. Mr. Justice Shears wrote :—

"As you will see, there is abundant intrinsic evidence that no native wrote it. My own idea, which I share with a good many people, is that it came from the pen of the Director of Education, which is as facile as it would very naturally be hostile. Let me know what you think. Ancram is non-committal, but he talks of Government's prosecuting the paper, which looks as if the article had already done harm."

Doyle went through the editorial with interest that increased as his eye travelled down the column. He smiled as he read; it was certainly a telling and a forcible presentation of the case against His Honour's policy, adorned with gibes that were more damaging than its argument. Suddenly he stopped, with a puzzled look, and read the last part of a sentence once again:—

"But he has a noble preference for the ideal of an impeccable Indian administrator, which he goes about contemplating, while his beard grows with the tale of his blunders."

The light of a sudden revelation twinkled in Doyle's eyes—a revelation which showed the Chief Secretary to the Bengal Government led on by vanity to forgetfulness. He reopened Ancram's letter, and convinced himself that the words were precisely those he had read there. For further assurance, he glanced at the dates of the letter and the newspaper: the one had been written two days before the other had been printed. Presently he put them down, and instinctively rubbed his thumb and the ends of his fingers together with the light, rapid movement with which people assure themselves that they have touched nothing soiling. He permitted himself no characterisation of the incident—lofty denunciation was not part of Doyle's habit of mind—beyond what might have been expressed in the somewhat disgusted smile with which he re-lighted his pipe. It was like him that his principal reflection had a personal tinge, and that it was forcible enough to find words. "And I," he said, with a twinkle at his own expense, "lived nine months in the same house with that skunk!"

CHAPTER XVI.

EVERY day at ten o'clock the south wind came hotter and stronger up from the sea. The sissoo trees on the Maidan trembled into delicate flower, and their faint, fresh fragrance stood like a spell about them. The teak pushed out its awkward rags, tawdry and foolish, but divinely green; and here and there a tamarind by the roadside lifted its gracious head, like a dream-tree in a billow of misty leaf. The days grew long and lovely; the coolies going home at sunset across the burnt grass of the Maidan joined hands and sang, with marigolds round their necks. The white-faced aliens of Calcutta walked there too, but silently, for "exercise." The crows grew noisier than ever, for it was young crow time; the fever-bird came and told people to put up their punkahs. The Viceroy and all that were officially his departed to Simla, and great houses in Chowringhee were to let. It was announced rather earlier than usual that His Honour the Lieutenant-Governor would go "on tour," which had no reference to Southern Europe, but meant inspection duty in remote parts of the province. Mrs. Church would accompany the Lieutenant-Governor. The local papers, in making this known, said it was hoped that the change of air would completely restore "one of Calcutta's most brilliant and popular hostesses," whose health for the past fortnight had been regrettably unsatisfactory.

The Dayes went to Darjiling, and Dr. MacInnes to England. Dr. MacInnes' expenses to England, and those of Shib Chunder Bhose, who accompanied him, were met out of a fund which had swelled astonishingly considering that it was fed by Bengali sentiment—the fund established to defeat the College Grants Notification. Dr. MacInnes went home, as one of the noble band of Indian missionaries, to speak to the people of England, and to explain to them how curiously the administrative mind in India became perverted in its conceptions of the mother country's duty to the heathen masses who look to her for light and guidance. Dr. MacInnes was prepared to say that the cause of Christian missions in India had been put back fifty years by the ill-judged act, so fearful in its ultimate consequences, of the Lieutenant-Governor of Bengal. Since that high official could not be brought to consider his responsibility to his Maker, he should be brought to consider his responsibility to the people of England. Dr. MacInnes doubtless did not intend to imply that the latter tribunal was the higher of the two, but he certainly produced the impression that it was the more effective.

Shib Chunder Bhose, in fluent and deferential language, heightened this impression, which did no harm to the cause. Shib Chunder Bhose had been found willing, in consideration of a second-class passage, to accompany Dr. MacInnes in the character of a University graduate who was also a Christian convert. Shib Chunder's father had married a Mohamedan woman, and so lost his caste, whereafter he embraced Christianity because Father Ambrose's predecessor had given him four annas every time he came to catechism. Shib Chunder inherited the paternal religion, with contumely added on the score of his mother, and, since he could make no' other pretension, figured in the College register as Christian. A young man anxious to keep pace with the times, he had been a Buddhist since, and afterwards professed his faith in the tenets of Theosophy; but whenever he fell ill or lost money he returned irresistibly to the procedure of his youth, and offered rice and marigolds to the Virgin Mary. Dr. MacInnes therefore certainly had the facts on his side when he affectionately referred to his young friend as living testimony to the work of educational missions in India, living proof of the falsity of the charge that the majority of mission colleges were mere secular institutions. As his young friend wore a frock-coat and a humble smile, and was able on occasion to weep like anything, the effect in the provinces was tremendous.

Dr. MacInnes gave himself to the work with a zeal which entirely merited the commendation he received from his conscience. Sometimes he lectured twice a day. He was always freely accessible to interviewers from the religious press. He refrained, in talking to these gentlemen, from all personal malediction of the Lieutenant-Governor—it was the sin he had to do with, not the distinguished sinner—and thereby gained a widespread reputation for unprejudiced views. Portraits of the reverend crusader and Shib Chunder Bhose appeared on the posters which announced Dr. MacInnes' subject in large letters—" MISSIONS AND MAMMON. SHALL A LIEUTENANT-GOVERNOR ROB GOD?"—and in all the illustrated papers. The matter arrived regularly with the joint at Hammersmith Sunday dinner-tables. Finally the *Times* gave it almost a parochial importance, and solemnly, in two columns, with due respect for constituted authority, came to no conclusion at all from every point of view.

The inevitable question was early asked in Parliament, and the Under-Secretary of State said he would "inquire." Further questions were asked on different and increasingly urgent grounds, with the object of reminding and hastening the Secretary of State. A popular Nonconformist preacher told two thousand people in Exeter Hall that they and he could no longer conscientiously vote to keep a Government in office that would hesitate to demand the instant resignation of an official who had brought such shame upon the name of England. Shortly afterwards one hon. member made a departure in his attack upon Mr. John Church, which completely held the attention of the House while it lasted. The effect was unusual, to be achieved by this particular hon. member, and he did it by reading aloud the whole of an extremely graphic and able article criticising His Honour's policy from the *Bengal Free Press*.

"I put it to hon. members," said he, weightily, in conclusion, "whether any one of us, in our boasted superiority of intellect, has the right to say that people who can thus express themselves do not know what they want!"

That evening, before he went to bed, Lord Strathell, Secretary of State for India, in Eaton Square, London, wrote a note to Lord Scansleigh, Viceroy and Governor-General of India, in Viceregal Lodge, Simla. The note was written on Lady Strathell's letter-paper, which was delicately scented and bore a monogram and coronet. It was a very private and friendly note, and it ran :—

"Dear Scansleigh : I needn't tell you how much I regret the necessity of my accompanying official letter asking you to arrange Church's retirement. I can quite understand that it will be most distasteful to you, as I know you have a high opinion of him, both personally and as an administrator. But the Missionary Societies, etc., have got us into the tightest possible place over his educational policy. Already several Nonconformist altars—if there are such things—are crying out for the libation of our blood. Somebody must be offered up. I had a Commission suggested, and it was received with rage and scorn. Nothing will do but Church's removal from his present office—and the sooner the better. I suppose we must find something else for him.

"Again assuring you of my personal regret, believe me, dear Scansleigh, yours cordially,

"Strathell.

" P.S.—Thus Party doth make Pilates of us all."

CHAPTER XVII.

It was the first time in history that the town of Bhugsi had been visited by a Lieutenant-Governor. Bhugsi was small, but it had a reputation for malodorousness not to be surpassed by any municipality of Eastern Bengal. Though Bhugsi was small it was full—full of men and children and crones and monkeys, and dwarfed, lean-ribbed cattle, and vultures of the vilest appetite. The town squatted round a tank, very old, very slimy, very sacred. Bhugsi bathed in the tank and so secured eternal happiness, drank from the tank and so secured it quickly. All such abominations as are unnameable Bhugsi also preferred to commit in the vicinity of the tank, and it was possibly for this reason that the highest death-rate of the last "year under report" had been humbly submitted by Bhugsi.

Noting this achievement, John Church added

Bhugsi to his inspection list. The inspection list was already sufficiently long for the time at his disposal, but Church had a way of economising his time that contributed much to the discipline of provincial Bengal. He accomplished this by train and boat and saddle; and his staff, with deep inward objurgations, did its best to keep up. He pressed upon Judith the advisability of a more leisurely progress by easier routes, with occasional meeting-places, but found her quietly obstinate in her determination to come with him. She declared herself the better for the constant change and the stimulus of quick moves; and this he could believe, for whenever they made a stay of more than forty-eight hours anywhere it was always she who was most feverishly anxious to depart. She filled her waking moments and dulled her pain in the natural way, with actual physical exertion. While the servants looked on in consternation she toiled instinctively over packings and unpackings, and was glad of the weariness they brought her. She invented little new devotions to her husband—these also soothed her—and became freshly solicitous about his health, freshly thoughtful about his comfort. Observing which, Church reflected tenderly on the unselfishness of women, and said to his wife that he could not have her throwing herself, this way, before the Juggernaut of his official progress.

There were no Europeans at all at Bhugsi, so the Lieutenant-Governor's party put up at the dâk-bungalow, three miles outside the town. Peter Robertson, the Commissioner of the Division, and the district officer, who were in attendance upon His Honour, were in camp near by, as their custom is. The dâk-bungalow had only three rooms, and this made the fact that two of His Honour's suite had been left at the last station with fever less of a misfortune. By this time, indeed, the suite consisted of Judith and the private secretary and the servants; but as John Church said, getting into his saddle at six o'clock in the morning, there were quite enough of them to terrify Bhugsi into certain reforms.

He spent three hours inspecting the work of the native magistrate, and came back to breakfast with his brows well set together over that official's amiable tolerance of a popular way of procuring confessions among the police, which was by means of needles and the supposed criminal's finger-nails. It had been practised in Bhugsi, as the native magistrate represented, for thousands of years, but it made Jöhn Church angry. He ate with stern eyes upon the table-cloth, and when the meal was over rode back to Bhugsi. There was only that one day, and beside the all-important matter of the sanitation he had to look at the schools, to inspect the gaol, to receive an address and to make a speech. He reflected on the terms of the speech as he rode, improving upon their salutary effect. He said to his private secretary, cantering alongside, that he had never known it so hot in April—the air was like a whip. It was borne in upon him once that if he could put down the burden of his work and of his dignity and stretch himself out to sleep beside the naked coolies who lay on their faces in the shadow of the pipal trees by the roadside, it would be a pleasant thing, but this he did not say to his private secretary.

It was half-past five, and the bamboos were all alive with the evening twitter of hidden sparrows, before the Lieutenant-Governor returned. For an instant Judith, coming out at the sound of hoofs, failed to recognise her husband, he looked, with a thick white powder of dust over his beard and eyebrows, so old a man. He stooped in his saddle, too, and all the gauntness of his face and figure had a deeper accent.

"Put His Honour to bed, Mrs. Church," cried the Commissioner, lifting his hat as he rode on to camp. "He has done the work of six men to-day."

"You will be glad of some tea," she said.

He tumbled clumsily out of his saddle and leaned for a moment against his animal's shoulder. The mare put her head round whinnying, but when Church searched in his pocket for her piece of sugar-cane and offered it to her, she snuffed it and refused it. He dropped the sugar-cane into the dust at her feet and told the syce to take her away.

"If she will not eat her gram give me word of it," he said. But she ate her gram.

"Will you change first, John?" Judith asked with her hand on his coat-sleeve. "I think you should—you are wet through and through."

"Yes, I will change," he said; but he dropped into the first chair he saw. The chair stood on the verandah, and the evening breeze had already begun to come up. He threw back his head and unfastened his damp collar and felt its gratefulness. In the intimate neighbourhood of the dâk-bungalow the private secretary could be heard splashing in his tub.

"Poor Sparks!" said His Honour. "I'm afraid he has had a hard day of it. Good fellow, Sparks, thoroughly good fellow. I hope he'll get on. It's very disheartening work, this of ours in India," he went on absently; "one feels the depression of it always, more or less, but to-night——" He paused and closed his eyes as if he were too weary to finish the sentence. A servant appeared with a wicker table and another with a tray.

"A cup of tea," said Judith cheerfully, "will often redeem the face of nature"; but he waved it back.

"I am too hungry for tea. Tell them to bring me a solid meal: cold beef—no, make it hot—that game pie we had at breakfast—anything there is, but as soon as possible. How refreshing this wind is!"

"Go and change, John," his wife urged.

"Yes, I must, immediately: I shall be taking a chill." As he half rose from his chair he saw the postman, turbaned, barefooted, crossing the grass from the road, and dropped back again.

"Here is the dâk," he said; "I must just have a look first."

Mrs. Church took her letters, and went into the house to give orders to the butler. Five minutes afterwards she came back, to find her husband sitting where she had left him, but upright in his chair and mechanically stroking his beard, with his face set. He had grown paler, if that was possible, but had lost every trace of lassitude. He had the look of being face to face with a realised contingency which his wife knew well.

"News, John?" she asked nervously; "anything important?"

"The most important—and the worst," he answered steadily, without looking at her. His eyes were fixed on the floor, and on his course of action.

"What do you mean, dear? What has happened? May I see?"

For answer he handed her his private letter from Lord Scansleigh. She opened it with shaking fingers, and read the first sentence or two aloud. Then instinctively her voice stopped, and she finished it in silence. The Viceroy had written :—

"MY DEAR CHURCH: The accompanying official correspondence will show you our position, when the mail left England, with the Secretary of State. I fear that nothing has occurred in the meantime to improve it—in fact, one or two telegrams seem rather to point the other way. I will not waste your time and mine in idle regrets, if indeed they would be justifiable, but write only to assure you heartily in private, as I do formally in my official letter, that if we go we go together. I have already telegraphed this to Strathell, and will let you know the substance of his reply as soon as I receive it. I wish I could think that the prospect of my own resignation is likely to deter them from demanding yours, but I own to you that I expect our joint immolation will not be too impressive a sacrifice for the British Public in this connection.

"With kind regards to Mrs. Church, in which my wife joins,

"Believe me, dear Church, yours sincerely,

"Scansleigh."

They spoke for a few minutes of the Viceroy's loyalty and consideration and appreciation. She dwelt upon that with instinctive tact, and then Church got up quickly.

"I must write to Scansleigh at once," he said. "I am afraid he is determined about this, but I must write. There is a great deal to do. When Sparks comes out send him to me." Then he went over to her and awkwardly kissed her. "You have taken it very well, Judith," he said—"better than any woman I know would have done."

She put a quick detaining hand upon his arm. "Oh, John, it is only for your sake that I care at all. I—I am so tired of it. I should be only too glad to go home with you, dear, and find some little place in the country where we could live quietly——"

"Yes, yes," he said, hurrying away. "We can discuss that afterwards. Don't keep Sparks talking."

Sparks appeared presently, swinging an embossed silver cylinder half a yard long. New washed and freshly clad in garments of clean country silk, with his damp hair brushed crisply off his forehead, there was a pinkness and a healthiness about Sparks that would have been refreshing at any other moment. "Have you seen this bauble, Mrs. Church?" he inquired: "Bhugsi's tribute, enshrining the address. It makes the fifth."

Judith looked at it, and back at Captain Sparks, who saw, with a falling countenance, that there were tears in her eyes.

"It is the last he will ever receive," she said, and one of the tears found its way down her cheek. "They have asked him from England to resign—they say he must."

Captain Sparks, private secretary, stood for a moment with his legs apart in blank astonishment, while Mrs. Church sought among the folds of her skirt for her pocket-handkerchief.

"By the Lord—impossible!" he burst out; and then, as Judith pointed mutely to her husband's room, he turned and shot in that direction, leaving her, as her sex is usually left, with the teacups and the situation.

.   .   .   .

A few hours later Captain Sparks' dreams of the changed condition of things were interrupted by a knock. It was Mrs. Church, sleepy-eyed, in her dressing-gown, with a candle; and she wanted the chlorodyne from the little travelling medicine chest, which was among the private secretary's things.

"My husband seems to have got a chill," she said. "It must have been while he sat in the verandah. I am afraid he is in for a wretched night."

"Three fingers of brandy," suggested Sparks concernedly, getting out the bottle. "Nothing like brandy."

"He has tried brandy. About twenty drops of this, I suppose?"

"I should think so. Can I be of any use?"

Judith said No, thanks—she hoped her husband would get some sleep presently. She went away, shielding her flickering candle, and darkness and silence came again where she had been.

A quarter of an hour later she came back, and it appeared that Captain Sparks could be of use. The chill seemed obstinate; they must rouse the servants and get fires made and water heated. Judith wanted to know how soon one might repeat the dose of chlorodyne. She was very much awake, and had that serious, pale decision with which women take action in emergencies of sickness.

Later still they stood outside the door of his room and looked at each other. "There is a European doctor at Bhai Gunj," said Captain Sparks. "He may be here with luck by six o'clock to-morrow afternoon—*this* afternoon." He looked at his watch and saw that it was past midnight. "Bundal Singh has gone for him, and Juddoo for the native apothecary at Bhugsi—but he will be useless. Robertson will be over immediately. He has seen cases of it, I know."

A thick sound came from the room they had left, and they hurried back into it.

* * * * * *

"Water?" repeated the Commissioner; "yes, as much as he likes. I wish to God we had some ice."

"Then, sir, I may take leave?" It was the unctuous voice of the native apothecary.

"No, you may not. Damn you, I suppose you can help to rub him? Quick, Sparks; the turpentine!"

* * * * * *

Next day at noon arrived Hari Lal, who had travelled many hours and many miles with a petition to the Chota Lât Sahib, wherein he and his village implored that the goats might eat the young shoots in the forest as aforetime; for if not —they were all poor men—how should the goats eat at all? Hari Lal arrived upon his beast, and saw from afar off that there was a chuprassie in red and gold upon the verandah whose favour would cost money. So he dismounted at a considerable and respectful distance, and approached humbly, with salaams and words that were suitable to a chuprassie in red and gold. The heat stood fiercely about the bungalow, and it was so silent that a pair of sparrows scolding in the verandah made the most unseemly wrangle.

Bundal Singh had not the look of business. He sat immovable upon his haunches, with his hands hanging between his knees. His head fell forward heavily, his eyes were puffed, and he regarded Hari Lal with indifference.

"O most excellent, how can a poor man seeking justice speak with the Lât Sahib? The matter is a matter of goats——"

"*Bus!* The Lât Sahib died in the little dawn. This place is empty but for the widow. *Mutti dani wasti gia*—they have gone to give the earth. It was the bad sickness, and the pain of it lasted only five hours. When he was dead, worthy one, his face was like a blue puggri that has been thrice washed, and his hand was no larger than the hand of my woman! What talk is there of justice? *Bus!*"

Hari Lal heard him through with a countenance that grew ever more terrified. Then he spat vigorously, and got again upon his animal. "And you, fool, why do you sit here?" he asked quaveringly, as he sawed at the creature's mouth.

"Because the servant-folk of the Sirkar do not run away. Who then would do justice and collect taxes, *budzat? Jao*, you Bengali rice-eater! I am of a country where those who are not women are men!"

The Bengali rice-eater went as he was bidden, and only a little curling cloud of white dust, sinking back into the road under the sun, remained to tell of him. Bundal Singh, hoarse with hours of howling, lifted up his voice in the silence because of the grief within him, and howled again.

A little wind stole out from under a clump of mango trees and chased some new-curled shavings about the verandah, and did its best to blow them in at the closed shutters of a darkened room. The shavings were too substantial, but the scent of the fresh-cut planks came through, and brought the stunned woman on the bed a sickening realisation of one unalterable fact in the horror of great darkness through which she groped, babbling prayers.

CHAPTER XVIII.

"IT was all very well for *him*, poor man, to want to be buried in that hole-and-corner kind of way—where he fell, I suppose, doing his duty: very simple and proper, I'm sure; and I should have felt just the same about it in his place— but on *her* account he ought to have made it possible for them to have taken him back to Calcutta and given him a public funeral."

Mrs. Daye spoke feelingly, gently tapping her egg. Mrs. Daye never could induce herself to cut off the top of an egg with one fell blow; she always tapped it, tenderly, first.

"It would have been something!" she continued. "Poor dear thing! I *was* so fond of Mrs. Church."

"I see they have started subscriptions to give him a memorial of sorts," remarked her husband from behind his newspaper. "But whether it's to be put in Bhugsi or in Calcutta doesn't seem to be arranged."

"Oh, in Calcutta, of course! They won't get fifty rupees if it's to be put up at Bhugsi. *Nobody* would subscribe!"

"Is there room?" asked Miss Daye meekly, from the other side of the table. "The illustrious are already so numerous on the Maidan. Is there no danger of overcrowding?"

"How ridiculous you are, Rhoda! You'll subscribe, Richard, of course? Considering how *very* kind they've been to us I should say— what do you think?—a hundred rupees." Mrs. Daye buttered her toast with knitted brows.

"We'll see. Hello! Spence is coming out again. 'By special arrangement with the India Office.' He's fairly well now, it seems, and willing to sacrifice the rest of his leave 'rather than put Government to the inconvenience of another possible change of policy in Bengal.' *That* means," Colonel Daye continued, putting down the Calcutta paper and taking up his coffee-cup, "that Spence has got his orders from Downing Street, and is being packed back to reverse this

College Grants business. But old Hawkins won't have much of a show, will he? Spence will be out in three weeks."

"I'm very pleased," Mrs. Daye remarked vigorously. "Mrs. Hawkins was bad enough in the Board of Revenue; she'd be un*bear*able at Belvedere. And Mrs. Church was so *per*fectly unaffected. But I don't think we would be quite justified in giving a hundred, Richard—seventy-five would be ample."

"One would think, mummie, that the hat was going round for Mrs. Church," said her daughter.

"Hats have gone round for less deserving persons," Colonel Daye remarked, "and in cases where there was less need of them, too. St. George writes me that there was no insurances, and not a penny saved. Church has always been obliged to do so much for his people. The widow's income will be precisely her three hundred a year of pension, and no more—bread and butter, but no jam."

"Talking of jam," said Mrs. Daye, with an effect of pathos, "if you haven't eaten it all,

Richard, I should like some. Poor dear thing! And if she marries again, she loses even that, doesn't she? Oh, no, she doesn't, either: there was that Madras woman that had three husbands and three pensions; they came altogether to nine hundred a year in the end. Of course, money is out of the question; but a little offering of something useful—made in a friendly way—she might even be grateful for. I am thinking of sending her a little something."

"What, mummie?" Rhoda demanded, with suspicion.

"That long black cloak I got when we all had to go into mourning for your poor dear grandmother, Rhoda. I've hardly worn it at all. Of course, it would require a little alteration, but——"

"*Mummie!* How beastly of you! You must not *dream* of doing it."

"It's fur-lined," said Mrs. Daye, with an injured inflection. "Besides, she isn't the wife of the L.G. *now*, you know."

" Papa——"

"What? Oh, certainly not! Ridiculous!

Besides, you're too late with your second-hand souvenir, my dear. St. George says that Mrs. Church sails to-day from Calcutta. Awfully cut up, poor woman, he says. Wouldn't go back to Belvedere; wouldn't see a soul: went to a boarding-house and shut herself up in two rooms."

"How un*kind* you are about news, Richard! Fancy your not telling us that before! And I think you and Rhoda are *quite* wrong about the cloak. If *you* had died suddenly of cholera in a a dâk-bungalow in the wilds and *I* was left with next to nothing, I would accept little presents from friends in the spirit in which they were offered, no matter *what* my position had been!"

"I daresay you would, my dear. But if I— hello! Exchange is going up again—if I catch you wearing cast-off mourning for me, I'll come and hang around until you burn it. By the way, I saw Doyle last night at the Club."

"The barrister? Did you speak to him?" asked Mrs. Daye.

"Yes. 'Hello!' I said: 'thought you were

on leave. What in the world brings you up here?' Seems that Pattore telegraphed askin' Doyle to defend him in this big diamond case with Ezra, and he came out. 'Well,' I said, 'Pattore's in Calcutta, Ezra's in Calcutta, diamond's in Calcutta, an' you're in Darjiling. When I'm sued for two lakhs over a stone to dangle on my tummy I won't retain you!'"

"And what did Mr. Doyle say to that, papa?" his daughter inquired.

"Oh—I don't remember. Something about never having seen the place before or something. Here, khansamah—cheroot!"

The man brought a box and lighted a match, which he presently applied to one end of the cigar while his master pulled at the other.

"Well," said Mrs. Daye, thoughtfully dabbling in her finger-bowl, "about this statue or whatever it is to Mr. Church—if it were a mere question of inclination—but as things are, Richard, I really don't think we can afford more than fifty. It isn't as if it could do the poor man any good. Where are you going, Rhoda? Wait a minute."

Mrs. Daye followed her daughter out of the room, shutting the door behind her, and put an impressive hand upon Rhoda's arm at the foot of the staircase.

"My dear child," she said, with a note of candid compassion, "what do you think has happened? Your father and I were discussing it as you came down, but I said 'Not a word before Rhoda!' They have made Lewis Ancram Chief Commissioner of Assam!"

The colour came back into the girl's face with a rush, and the excitement went out of her eyes.

"Good heavens, mummie, how you—— Why shouldn't they? Isn't he a proper person?"

"Very much so. *That* has nothing to do with it. Think of it, Rhoda—a Chief Commissioner, at his age! And you *can't* say I didn't prophesy it. *The* rising man in the Civil Service I always told you he was."

"And I never contradicted you, mummie dear! My own opinion is that when Abdur Rahman dies they'll make him Amir!" Rhoda laughed a gay, irresponsible laugh, and tripped on upstairs with singular lightness of step. Mrs. Daye, leaning upon the end of the banister, followed her with reproachful eyes.

"You seem to take it very lightly, Rhoda, but I must say it serves you perfectly right for having thrown the poor man over in that disgraceful way. Girls who behave like that are generally sorry for it later. I knew of a chit here in Darjiling that jilted a man in the Staff Corps and ran away with a tea-planter. The man will be the next Commander-in-Chief of the Indian Army, everybody says, and I hope she likes her tea-planter."

"Mummie!" Rhoda called down confidentially from the landing.

"Well?"

"Put your head in a bag, mummie. I'm going out. Shall I bring you some chocolates or some nougat or anything?"

"I shall tell your father to whip you. Yes, chocolates if they're fresh—*insist* upon that. Those crumbly Neapolitan ones, in silver-and-gold paper."

"All right. And mummie!"

"What?"

"Write and congratulate Mr. Ancram. Then he'll know there's no ill-feeling!"

Which Mrs. Daye did.

CHAPTER XIX.

TEN minutes later Rhoda stood fastening her glove at her father's door and looking out upon a world of suddenly novel charm. The door opened, as it were, upon eternity,. with a patch of garden between, but eternity was blue and sun-filled and encouraging. The roses and sweet-williams stood sheer against the sky, with fifty yellow butterflies dancing above them. Over the verge of the garden—there was not more than ten feet of it in any direction—she saw tree-tops and the big green shoulders of the lower hills, and very far down a mat of fleecy clouds that hid the flanks of some of these. The sunlight was tempting, enticing. It made the rubble path warm beneath her feet and drew up the scent of the garden until the still air palpitated with it. Rhoda took little desultory steps to the edge of the ledge the house was built on, and down the steep footway to the road. The white oaks met over her head, and far up among the tree-ferns she heard a cuckoo. Its note softened and accented her unreasoned gladness, seemed to give it a form and a metre. She looked up into the fragrant leafy shadows and listened till it came again, vaguely aware that it was enough to live for. If she had another thought it was that Philip Doyle had come too late to see the glory of the rhododendrons, there was only, here and there, a red rag of them left.

She stepped with a rattle of pebbles into the wide main road round the mountain, and there stood for a moment undecided. It was the chief road, the Mall; and if she turned to the right it would lead her past the half-dozen tiny European shops that clung to the side of the hill, past the hotels and the club, and through the expansion where the band played in the afternoon, where there were benches and an admirable view, and where new-comers to Darjiling invariably sat for two or three days and contentedly occupied themselves with processes of oxygenation. This part of the Mall was frequented and fashionable; even at that hour she would meet her acquaintances on hill ponies and her mother's friends in dandies and her mother's friends' babies in perambulators, with a plentiful background of slouching Bhutia coolies, their old felt hats tied on with their queues, and red-coats from a recuperating regiment, and small black-and-white terriers. It was not often that this prospect attracted her; she had discovered a certain monotony in its cheerfulness some time before; but to-day she had to remind herself of that discovery before she finally decided to turn to the left instead. She had another reason: if she went that way it might look to Philip Doyle as if she wanted to meet him. Why this gentleman should have come to so extraordinary a conclusion on the data at his disposal Miss Daye did not pause to explain. She was quite certain that he would, so she turned to the left.

It suited her mood, when once she had taken that direction, to walk very fast. She had an undefined sense of keeping pace with events; her vigorous steps made a rhythm for her buoyant thought, and helped it out. She was entirely occupied with the way in which she would explain to Mr. Doyle how it was that she was not married to Lewis Ancram. She anticipated a pleasure in this, and she thought it was because Doyle would be gratified, on his friend's account. He had never liked the match —she clung to that impression in all humility— he would perhaps approve of her breaking it off. Rhoda felt a little excited satisfaction at the idea of being approved of by Philip Doyle. She put the words with which she would tell him into careful phrases as she walked, constructing and reconstructing them, while Buzz kept an erratic course before her with inquisitive pauses by the wayside and vain chasing of little striped squirrels that whisked about the boles of the trees. Buzz, she thought, had never been more idiotically amusing.

The road grew boskier and lonelier. Miss Daye met a missionary lady in a jinricksha, and then a couple of schoolboys sprinting, and then for a quarter of a mile nobody at all. The little white houses stopped cropping out on ledges above her head, the wall of rock or of rubble rose solidly up, wet and glistening, and tapestried thick with tiny ferns and wild begonias. All at once, looking over the brink, she saw that the tin roofs of the cottages down the khud-side no longer shone in the sun; the clouds had rolled between it and them—very likely down there it was raining. Presently the white mist smoked up level with the road, and she and the trees and the upper mountain stood in dappled sunlight for a moment alone above a phantasmally submerged world. Then the crisp leaf-shadows on the road grew indistinct and faded, the sunlight paled and went out, and in a moment there was nothing near or far but a wandering greyness, and here and there perhaps the shadowed bole of an oak-tree or the fantastic outline of a solitary nodding fern.

"It's going to rain, Buzz," she said, as the little dog mutely inquired for encouragement and direction, "and neither of us have got an umbrella. So we'll both get wet and take our death of cold. *Sumja,** Buzz?"

As she spoke they passed the blurred figure of a man, walking rapidly in the other direction. "Buzz!" Rhoda cried, as the dog turned and trotted briskly after: "Come back, sir!" Buzz took no notice whatever, and immediately she heard him addressed in a voice which made a sudden requirement upon her self-control. She had a divided impulse—to betake herself on as fast as she could into remote indistinguishability, and to call the dog again. With a little effort of hardihood she turned and called him, turned with a thumping heart, and waited for his restoration and for anything else that might happen. The mist drifted up for a moment as Philip Doyle heard her and came quickly back; and when they shook hands they stood in a little white temple with uncertain walls and a ceiling decoration of tree-ferns in high relief.

She asked him when he had come, although she knew that already, and he inquired for her

---

* "Do you understand?"

mother, although he was quite informed as to Mrs. Daye's well-being. He explained Buzz's remembering him, as if he had taken an unfair advantage of it, and they announced simultaneously that it was going to rain. Then conversation seemed to fail them wholly, and Rhoda made a movement of departure.

"I suppose you are going to some friend in the neighbourhood," he said, lifting his hat, "if there is any neighbourhood—which one is inclined to doubt."

"Oh, no, I'm only walking."

"All alone?"

"Buzz," she said, with a downcast smile.

"Buzz is such an effective protection that I'm inclined to ask you to share him." His voice was even more tentative than his words. He fancied he would have made a tremendous advance if she allowed him to come with her.

"Oh, yes," she said foolishly, "you may have half."

"Thank you. I am three miles from my club, twenty-four hours from my office, and four thousand feet above sea-level—and I don't mind confessing that I'm very frightened indeed. How long, I wonder, does it take to acquire the magnificent indifference to the elements which you display? But the storm is indubitably coming: don't you think we had better turn back?"

"Yes," she said again, and they turned back; but they sauntered along among the clouds at precisely the pace they might have taken in the meadows of the world below.

She asked him where he had spent his leave and how he had enjoyed it, and she gathered from his replies that one might stay too long in India to find even Italy wholly paradisaical, although Monte Carlo had always its same old charm. "You should see Monte Carlo before some cataclysm overtakes it," he said. "You would find it amusing. I spent a month at Homburg," he went on humorously, "with what I consider the greatest possible advantage to my figure. Though my native friends have been openly condoling with me on my consequent loss of prestige, and I have no doubt my sylph-like condition will undermine my respectability."

He felt, as he spoke, deplorably middle-aged, and to mention these things seemed to be a kind of apology for them.

Rhoda looked at him with the conviction that he had left quite ten years in Europe, but she found herself oddly reluctant to say so. "Mummie will tell you," she said. "Mummie always discovers the most wonderful changes in people when they have been home. And why did you come back so soon?"

"Why?" he repeated, half facing round, and then suddenly dropping back again. "I came to see about something."

"Oh, yes, of course you did. I know about it. And do you think you will win?"

She looked at him with a smile of timid intelligence. Under it she was thinking that she had never had such a stupid conversation with Mr. Doyle before. He smiled back gravely, and considered for a moment.

"I don't in the least know," he said with courageous directness; "but I mean to try—very hard."

If he had thought, he might have kept the suggestion out of his voice—it was certainly a little premature—but he did not think, and the suggestion was there. Rhoda felt her soul leap up to catch its full significance; then she grew very white, and shivered a little. The shiver was natural enough: two or three big drops had struck her on the shoulders, and others were driving down upon the road, with wide spaces between them, but heavily determined, and making little splashes where they struck.

"It is going to pour," she said; and, as they walked on with a futile quickening of pace, she heard him talk of something else, and called herself a fool for the tumult in her heart. The rain gathered itself together and pelted them. She was glad of the excuse to break blindly into a run, and Doyle needed all his newly acquired energy to keep up with her. The storm was behind them, and as it darkened and thickened and crashed and drove them on, Rhoda's blood tingled with a wild sweet knowledge that she fled before something stronger and stranger than the storm, and that in the end she would be overtaken, in the end she would cede. Her sense of this culminated when Philip Doyle put a staying hand upon her arm—she could not have heard him speak—and she sped on faster, with a little frightened cry.

"Come back!" he shouted; and, without knowing why, she did as he bade her, struggling at every step, it seemed, into a chaos out of which the rain smote her on both cheeks, with only one clear sensation—that he had her hand very closely pressed to his side, and that somewhere or other, presently, there would be shelter. They found it not ten yards behind— one of those shallow caves that Sri Krishna scooped out long ago to lodge his beggar priests in. Some Bhutia coolies had been cooking a meal there; a few embers still glowed on a heap of ashes in the middle of the place. Doyle explained, as he thrust her gently in, that these had caught his eye.

"You won't mind my leaving you here," he said, "while I go on for a dandy and wraps and things? I shall not be a moment longer than I can help. You won't be afraid?"

"In this rain! It would be wicked. Yes, I shall—I shall be horribly afraid! You must stay here too, until it is over. Please come inside *at once.*"

The little imperious note thrilled Doyle; but he stayed where he was.

"My dear child," he said, "this may last for hours, and, if you don't get home somehow, you are bound to get a chill. Besides, I must let your mother know."

"It will probably be over by the time you reach the house. And my mother is always quite willing to entrust me to Providence, Mr. Doyle. And if you go I'll come, too."

She looked so resolute that Doyle hesitated. "Won't you be implored to stay here?" he asked.

She shook her head. "Not if you go," she said. And, without further parley, he stooped and came in.

They could not stand upright against the shelving sides and roof of the place, so perforce they sat upon the ground—she, with her feet tucked under her, leaning upon one hand, in the way of her sex, he hugging his knees. There might have been thirty cubic feet of space in the cave, but it was not comfortably apportioned, and he had to crouch rather awkwardly to keep himself at what he considered a proper distance. It was warm and dry there, and the dull fire of the embers in the middle gave a centre and a significance to the completeness of their shelter. The clouds hung like a grey curtain before the entrance, bordered all round with trailing vines and drooping ferns; the beat of the rain came in to them in a heavy distant monotone, and even the thunder seemed to be rolling in a muffled way among the valleys below. Doyle felt that nothing could be more perfect than their solitude. He would not speak, lest his words should people it with commonplaces; he almost feared to move, lest he should destroy the accident that gave him the privilege of such closeness to her. The little place was filled, it seemed to him, with a certain divine exhalation of her personality, of her freshness and preciousness; he breathed it, and grew young again, and bold. In the moments of silence that fell their love arose before them like a presence. The girl saw how beautiful it was without looking, the man asked himself how long he could wait for its realisation.

"Are you very wet?" he asked her at last.

"No; only my jacket."

"Then you ought to take it off, oughtn't you? Let me help you."

He had to lean closer to her for that. The wet little coat came off with difficulty; and then he put an audacious hand upon the warm shoulder in its cambric blouse underneath, with a suddenly taught confidence that it would not shrink away.

"Only a little damp," he said. It was the most barefaced excuse for his caressing fingers. "Tell me, darling, when a preposterously venerable person like me wishes to make a proposal of marriage to somebody who is altogether sweet and young and lovable like you, has he any business to take advantage of a romantic situation to do it in?"

She did not answer. The lightness of his words somewhat disturbed her sense of their import. Then she looked into his face, and saw the wonderful difference that the hope of her had written there, and, without any more questioning, she permitted herself to understand.

"Think about it for a little while," he said, and came a good deal nearer, and drew her head down upon his breast. He knew a lifetime of sweet content in the space it rested there, while he laid his lips softly upon her hair and made certain that no other woman's was so sweet-scented.

"Well?" he said at last.

"But——"

"But?"

"But you never did approve of me."

"Didn't I? I don't know. I have always loved you."

"I have never loved anybody—before."

That was as near as she managed to get, then or for long thereafter, to the matter of her previous engagement.

"No. Of course not. But for the future?"

Without taking her head from his shoulder, she lifted her eyes to his; and he found the pledge he sought in them.

And that upturning of her face brought her

lips, her newly grave, sweet, submissive lips, very near, and the gladness within him was new-born and strong. And so the storm swept itself away, and the purple-necked doves cooed and called again where the sunlight glistened through the dripping laurels, and these two were hardly aware. Then suddenly a Bhutia girl with a rose behind her ear came and stood in the door of the cave and regarded them. She was muscular and red-cheeked and stolid; she wore many strings of beads as well as the rose behind her ear, and as she looked she comprehended, with a slow and foolish smile.

"It is her tryst!" Rhoda cried, jumping up. "Let us leave it to her."

Then they went home through a world of their own, which the piping birds and the wild roses and the sun-decked mosses reflected fitly. The clouds had gone to Thibet; all round about, in full sunlight, the great encompassing, gleaming Snows rose up and spoke of eternity, and made a horizon not too solemn and supreme for the vision of their happiness.

. . . . . .

"My dearest child," said Mrs. Daye that night—she had come late to her daughter's room with her hair down—"don't think I'm not as pleased as possible, because I *am*. I've always had the greatest admiration for Mr. Doyle, and you couldn't have a better—unofficial—position in Calcutta. But I *must* warn you, dear—I've seen such misfortune come of it, and I knew I shouldn't sleep if I didn't—before this engagement is announced——"

"I'll go to church in a cotton blouse and a serge skirt this time, if that's what you're thinking of, mummie."

"There! I was sure of it! Do think *seriously*, Rhoda, of the injustice to poor Mr. Doyle, if you're merely marrying him for *pique!*"

CHAPTER XX.

THE Honourable Mr. Ancram found himself gratified by Mrs. Church's refusal to see him in Calcutta. It filled out his idea of her, which was a delicate one, and it gave him a pleasurable suggestive of the stimulus which he should always receive from her in future toward the alternative which was most noble and most satisfying. Mr. Ancram had the clearest perception of the value of such stimulus; but the probability that he was likely to be able to put it permanently at his disposal could hardly be counted chief among the reasons which made him, at this time, so exceedingly happy. His promotion had even less to do with it. India is known to be full of people who would rather be a Chief Commissioner than Rudyard Kipling or Saint Michael, but this translation had been in the straight line of Mr. Ancram's intention for years; it offered him no fortuitous joy, and if it made a basis for the more refined delight which had entered his experience, that is as much as it can be credited with. Life had hitherto offered him no satisfaction that did not pale beside the prospect of possessing Judith Church. He gave dreamy half-hours to the realisation of how the sordidness of existence would vanish when he should regard it through her eyes, of how her goodness would sweeten the world to him, and her gaiety brighten it, and her beauty etherealise it. He tried to analyse the completeness of their fitness for each other, and invariably gave it up to fall into a little trance of longing and of anticipation.

He could not be sufficiently grateful to John Church for dying—it was a circumstance upon which he congratulated himself frankly, an accident by which he was likely to benefit so vastly that he could indulge in no pretence of regretting it on any altruistic ground. It was so decent of Church to take himself out of the way that his former Chief Secretary experienced a change of attitude toward him. Ancram still considered him an ass, but hostility had faded out of the opinion, which, when he mentioned it, dwelt rather upon that animal's power of endurance and other excellent qualities. Ancram felt himself distinctly on better terms with the late Lieutenant-Governor, and his feeling was accented by the fact that John Church died in time to avoid the necessity for a more formal resignation. His Chief Secretary felt personally indebted to him for that, on ethical grounds.

In the long, suggestive, caressing letters which reached Judith by every mail, he made an appearance of respecting her fresh widowhood that was really clever, considering the fervency which he contrived to imply. As the weeks went by, however, he began to consider this attitude of hers, the note she had struck in going six thousand miles away without seeing him, rather an extravagant gratification of conscience, and if she had been nearer it may be doubted whether his tolerance would have lasted. But she was in London and he was in Assam, which made restraint easier; and he was able always to send her the assurance of his waiting passion without hurting her with open talk of the day when he should come into his own. Judith, seeing that his pen was in a leash, watered her love anew with the thought of his innate nobility, and shortened the time that lay between them.

In spite of her conscience, which was a good one, there were times when Mrs. Church was shocked by the realisation that she was only trying to believe herself unhappy. In spite of other things, too, of a more material sort. Misfortune had overtaken the family at Stoneborough: ill-health had compelled her father to resign the pulpit of Beulah Church, and to retire upon a microscopic stipend from the superannuation fund. There was a boy of fourteen, much like his sister, who wanted to be a soldier, and did not want to wear a dirty apron and sell the currants of the leading member of his father's congregation. For these reasons Judith's three hundred a year shrank to a scanty hundred and fifty. The boy went to Clifton, and she to an attic in that south side of Kensington where they are astonishingly cheap. Here she established herself, and grew familiar with the devices of poverty. It was not picturesque Bohemian poverty; she had little ladylike ideals in gloves and shoes that she pinched herself otherwise to attain, and it is to be feared that she preferred looking shabby-genteel with eternal limitations to looking disreputable with spasmodic extravagances. But neither the sordidness of her life nor the discomfort she tried to conjure out of the past made her miserable. Rather she extracted a solace from them—they gave her a vague feeling of expiation; she hugged her little miseries for their purgatorial qualities, and felt, though she never put it into a definite thought, that they made a sort of justification for her hope of heaven.

Besides, except once a week, on Indian mail day, her life was for the time in abeyance. She had a curious sense occasionally, in some sordid situation to which she was driven for the lack of five shillings, of how little anything mattered during this little colourless period; and she declined kindly invitations from old Anglo-Indian acquaintances in more expensive parts of Kensington with almost an ironical appreciation of their inconsequence. She accepted existence without movement or charm for the time, since she could not dispense with it altogether. She invented little monotonous duties and occupied herself with then, and waited, always with the knowledge that just beyond her dingy horizon lay a world, her old world, of full life and vivid colour and long dramatic days, if she chose to look.

On mail days she did look, over Ancram's luxurious pages with soft eyes and a little participating smile. They made magic carpets for her—they had imaginative touches. They took her to the scent of the food-stuff in the chaffering bazar; she saw the white hot sunlight sharp-shadowed by dusty palms, and the people, with their gentle ways and their simplicity of guile, the clanking silver anklets of the coolie women, the black *kol* smudges under the babies' eyelashes—the dear people! She remembered how she had seen the oxen treading out the corn in the warm leisure of that country, and the women grinding at the mill. She remembered their simple talk; how the gardener had told her in his own tongue that the flowers ate much earth; how a syce had once handed her a beautiful bazar-written letter, in which he asked for more wages because he could not afford himself. She remembered the jewelled Rajahs, and the ragged magicians, and the coolies' song in the evening, and the home-trotting little oxen painted in pink spots in honour of a plaster goddess, and realised how she loved India. She realised it even more completely, perhaps, when November came and brought fogs which were always dreary in that they interfered with nothing that she wanted to do, and neuralgia that was especially hard to bear for being her only occupation. The winter dragged itself away. Beside Ancram's letters and her joy in answering them, she had one experience of pleasure keen enough to make it an episode. She found it in the *Athenian*, which she picked up on a news-stall, where she had dropped into the class of customers who glance over three or four weeklies and buy one or two. It was a review, a review of length and breadth and weight and density, of the second volume of the "Modern Influence of the Vedic Books," by Lewis Ancram, I.C.S. She bought the paper and took it home, and all that day her heart beat higher with her woman's ambition for the man she loved, sweetened with the knowledge that his own had become as nothing to the man who loved her.

CHAPTER XXI.

It was a foregone conclusion in Calcutta that the name of the Chief Commissioner of Assam should figure prominently in the Birthday Honours of the season. On the 24th of that very hot May people sat in their verandahs in early morning dishabille, and consumed tea and toast and plantains, and read in the local extras that a Knight Commandership of the Star of India had fluttered down upon the head of Mr. Lewis Ancram, without surprise. Doubtless the "Modern Influence of the Vedic Books" was to be reckoned with to some extent in the decorative result, but the general public gave it less importance than Sir Walter Besant, for example, would be disposed to do. The general public reflected rather upon the Chief Commissioner's conspicuous usefulness in Assam, especially the dexterity with which he had trapped border raids upon tea-plantations. The general public remembered how often it had seen Mr. Lewis Ancram's name in the newspapers, and in what invariably approved connections. So the men in pyjamas on the verandahs languidly regarded the wide flat spreading red-and-yellow bouquets of the gold mohur trees where the crows were gasping and swearing on the Maidan, and declared, with unanimous yawns, that Ancram was "just the fellow to get it."

The Supreme Government at Simla was even better acquainted with Lewis Ancram's achievements and potentialities than the general public, however. There had been occasions, when Mr. Ancram was a modest Chief Secretary only, upon which the Supreme Government had cause to congratulate itself privately as to Mr. Ancram's extraordinary adroitness in political moves affecting the "advanced" Bengali. Since his triumph over the College Grants Notification the advanced Bengali had become increasingly outrageous. An idea in this connection so far emerged from official representations at headquarters as to become almost obvious, as to leave no alternative—which is a very remarkable thing in the business of the Government of India. It was to the effect that the capacity to outwit the Bengali should be the single indispensable qualification of the next Lieutenant-Governor of Bengal.

"No merely straightforward chap will do," said Lord Scansleigh, with a sigh, "however able he may be. Of course," he added, "I don't mean to say that we want a crooked fellow, but our man must understand crookedness and be equal to it. That, poor Church never was."

The Viceroy delivered himself thus because Sir Griffiths Spence's retirement was imminent, and he had his choice for Bengal to make over again. Simplicity and directness apparently disqualified a number of gentleman of seniority and distinction, for ten days later it was announced that the appointment had fallen to Sir Lewis Ancram, K.C.S.I. Again the little world of Calcutta declined to be surprised: nothing, apparently, exceeded the popular ambition for the Chief Commissioner of Assam. Hawkins, of the Board of Revenue, was commiserated for a day or two, but it was very generally admitted that men like Hawkins of the Board of Revenue, solid, unpretentious fellows like that, were extremely apt, somehow, to be overlooked. People said generally that Scansleigh had done the right thing—that Ancram would know how to manage the natives. It was perceived that the new King of Bengal would bring a certain picturesqueness to the sceptre, he was so comparatively young and so superlatively clever. In view of this the feelings of Hawkins of the Board of Revenue were lost sight of. And nothing could have been more signal than the approbation of the native newspapers. Mohendra Lal Chuckerbutty, in the *Bengal Free Press*, wept tears of joy in leading articles every day for a week. " Bengal," said Mohendra, editorially, " has been given a man after her own heart." By which Sir Lewis Ancram was ungrateful enough to be annoyed.

Judith grew very white over the letter which brought her the news, remembering many things. It was a careful letter, but there was a throb of triumph in it—a suggestion, just perceptible, of the dramatic value of the situation. She told herself that this was inevitable and natural, just as inevitable and natural as all the rest; but at the same time she felt that her philosophy was not quite equal to the remarkable completeness of Ancram's succession. With all her pride in him, in her heart of hearts she would infinitely have preferred to share some degradation with him rather than this; she would have liked the taste of any bitterness of his misfortune better than this perpetual savour of his usurpation. It was a mere phase of feeling, which presently she put aside, but for the moment her mind dwelt with curious insistence upon one or two little pictorial memories of the other master of Belvedere, while tears stood in her eyes and a foolish resentment at this fortunate turn of destiny tugged at her heart-strings. In a little while she found herself able to rejoice for Ancram with sincerity, but all day she involuntarily recurred, with deep, gentle irritation, to the association of the living idea and the dead one.

Perhaps the liveliest pang inflicted by Sir

Lewis Ancram's appointment was experienced by Mrs. Daye. Mrs. Daye confided to her husband that she never saw the Belvedere carriage, with its guard of Bengal cavalry trotting behind, without thinking that if things had turned out differently she might be sitting in it, with His Honour her son-in-law. From which the constancy and keenness of Mrs. Daye's regrets may be in a measure inferred. She said to privileged intimate friends that she knew she was a silly, worldly thing, but really it did bring out one's silliness and worldliness to have one's daughter jilt a Lieutenant-Governor, in a way that nobody could understand whose daughter hadn't done it. Mrs. Daye took what comfort she could out of the fact that this limitation excluded every woman she knew. She would add, with her brow raised in three little wrinkles of deprecation, that of course they were immensely pleased with Rhoda's ultimate choice: Mr. Doyle was a dear, sweet man, but she, Mrs. Daye, could not help having a sort of sisterly regard for him, which towards one's son-in-law was ridiculous. He certainly had charming manners—the very man to appreciate a cup of tea and one's poor little efforts at conversation—if he didn't happen to be married to one's daughter. It was ludicrously impossible to have a seriously enjoyable *tête-à-tête* with a man who was married to one's daughter!

CHAPTER XXII.

CALCUTTA, when the Doyles came down from Darjiling, chased by the early rains, was prepared to find the marriage ridiculous. Calcutta counted on its fingers the years that lay between Mr. and Mrs. Doyle, and mentioned, as a condoning fact, that Philip Doyle's chances for the next High Court Judgeship were very good indeed. Following up this line of fancy, Calcutta pictured a matron growing younger and younger and a dignitary of the Bench growing older and older, added the usual accessories of jewels and balls and Hill captains and the private *entrée*, and figured out the net result, which was regrettably vulgar and even more regrettably common. It is perhaps due to Calcutta rather than to the Doyles to say that six weeks after their arrival these prophecies had been forgotten and people went about calling it an ideal match. One or two ladies went so far as to declare that Rhoda Daye had become a great deal more tolerable since her marriage; her husband was so much cleverer than she was, and that was what she needed, you know. In which statement might occasionally be discerned a gleam of satisfaction.

It shortly became an item of gossip that very few engagements were permitted to interfere with Mrs. Philip Doyle's habit of driving to her husband's office to pick him up at five o'clock in the afternoon, and that very few clients were permitted to keep him there after she had arrived. People smiled in indulgent comment on it, as the slender, light, tasteful figure in the cabriolet drove among the thronging carriages in the Red Road towards Old Post-Office Street, and looked again, with that paramount interest in individuals which is almost the only one where Britons congregate in exile. Mrs. Doyle, in the picturesque exercise of the domestic virtues, was generally conceded to be even more piquant than Miss Daye in the temporary possession of a Chief Secretary.

I have no doubt that on one special Wednesday afternoon she was noted to look absent and a trifle grave, as the Waler made his own pace to bring his master. There was no reason for this in particular, except that His Honour the Lieutenant-Governor was leaving for England by the mail train for Bombay that evening. Perhaps this in itself would hardly have sufficed to make Mrs. Doyle meditative, but there had been a great clamour of inquiry and suggestion as to why Sir Lewis Ancram was straining a point to obtain three months' leave under no apparent emergency: people said he had never looked better—and Mrs. Doyle believed she knew precisely why. The little cloud of her secret knowledge was before her eyes as the crows pecked hoarsely at the street offal under the Waler's deliberate feet, and she was somewhat impatient at being burdened with any acquaintance with Sir Lewis Ancram's private intentions. Also she remembered her liking for the woman he was going home to marry; and, measuring in fancy Judith Church's capacity for happiness, she came to the belief that it was likely to be meagrely filled. It was the overflowing measure of her own, perhaps, that gave its liveliness to her very real pang of regret. She knew Lewis Ancram so much better than Mrs. Church did, she assured herself; was it not proof enough, that the other woman loved him while she (Rhoda) bowed to him? As at that moment, when he passed her on horseback, looking young and vigorous and elate. Rhoda fancied a certain significance in his smile; it spoke of good-fellowship and the prospect of an equality of bliss and the general expediency of things as they were rather than as they might have been. She coloured hotly under it, and gathered up the reins and astonished the Waler with the whip.

As she turned into Old Post-Office Street, a flanking battalion of the rains—riding up dark and thunderous behind the red-brick turrets of the High Court—whipped down upon the Maidan, and drove her, glad of a refuge, up the dingy stairs to her husband's office. Her custom was to sit in the cabriolet and despatch the syce with a message. The syce would deliver it in his own tongue—" The memsahib sends a salutation "—and Doyle would presently appear. But to-day it was raining and there was no alternative.

A little flutter of consideration greeted her entrance. Two or three native clerks shuffled to their feet and salaamed, and one ran to open the door into Doyle's private room for her. Her husband sat writing against time at a large desk littered thick with papers. At another table a native youth in white cotton draperies sat making quill pens, with absorbed precision. The punkah swung a slow discoloured petticoat above them both. The tall wide windows were open. Through them little damp gusts came in and lifted the papers about the room; and beyond them the grey rain slanted down, and sobered the vivid green of everything, and turned the tilted palms into the likeness of draggled plumes waving against the sky.

"You have just escaped the shower," said Doyle, looking up with quick pleasure at her step. "I'll be another twenty minutes, I'm afraid. And I have nothing for you to play with," he added, glancing round the dusty room—" not even a novel. You must just sit down and be good."

"Mail letters?" asked Rhoda, with her hand on his shoulder.

The clerk was looking another way, and she dropped a foolish, quick little kiss on the top of his head.

"Yes. It's this business of the memorial to Church. I've got the newspaper reports of the unveiling together, and the Committee have drafted a formal letter to Mrs. Church, and there's a good deal of private correspondence —letters from big natives sending subscriptions, and all that—that I thought she would like to see. As Secretary to the Committee, it of course devolves upon me to forward everything. And at this moment," Doyle went on, glancing ruefully at the page under his hand, "I am trying to write to her privately, poor thing."

Rhoda glanced down at the letter. "I know you will be glad to have these testimonials, which are as sincere as they are spontaneous, to the unique position Church held in the regard of many distinguished people," she read deliberately, aloud.

"Do you think that is the right kind of thing to say? It strikes me as rather formal. But one is so terribly afraid of hurting her by some stupidity."

"Oh, I don't think so at all, Philip. I mean —it is quite the proper thing, I think. After all, it's—it's more than a year ago, you know."

"The wives of men like Church remember them longer than that, I fancy. But if you will be pleased to sit down, Mrs. Doyle, I'll finish it in some sort of decency and get it off."

Rhoda sat down and crossed her feet and looked into dusty vacancy. The recollection of Ancram's expression as he passed her in the road came back to her, and as she reflected that the ship which carried him to Judith Church would also take her the balm respectfully prepared by the Committee, her sense of humour curved her lips in an ironical smile. The grotesqueness of the thing made it seem less serious, and she found quite five minutes' interested occupation in considering it. Then she regarded the baboo making pens, and picked up a "Digest" and put it down again, and turned over the leaves of a tome on the "Hindu Law of Inheritance," and yawned, and looked out of the window, and observed that it had stopped raining.

"Philip, aren't you nearly done? Remember me affectionately to Mrs. Church—no, perhaps you'd better not, either."

Doyle was knitting his brows over a final sentiment, and did not reply.

"Philip, is that one of your old coats hanging on the nail? Is it old enough to give away? I want an old coat for the syce to sleep in: he had fever yesterday."

Mrs. Doyle went over to the object of her inquiries, took it down, and daintily shook it.

"*Philip!* Pay some attention to me. May I have this coat? There's nothing in the pockets —nothing but an old letter and a newspaper. Oh!"

Her husband looked up at last, noting a change in the tone of her exclamation. She stood looking in an embarrassed way at the address on the envelope she held. It was in Ancram's handwriting.

"What letter?" he asked.

She handed it to him, and at the sight of it he frowned a little.

"Is the newspaper the *Bengal Free Press?*"

"Yes," she said, glancing at it. "And it's marked in one or two places with red pencil."

"Then read them both," Doyle replied. "They don't tell a very pretty story, but it may amuse you. I thought I had destroyed them long ago. I can't have worn that coat since I left Florence."

Rhoda sat down, with a beating curiosity, and applied herself to understand the story that was not very pretty. It sometimes annoyed her that she could not resist her interest in things that concerned Ancram, especially things that exemplified him. She brought her acutest intelligence to bear upon the exposition of the letter and the newspaper; but it was very plain and simple, especially where it was underscored in red pencil, and she comprehended it at once. She sat thinking of it, with bright eyes, fitting it into relation with what she had known and guessed before, perhaps unconsciously pluming herself a little upon her penetration, and, it must be confessed, feeling a keen thrill of unregretting amusement at Ancram's conviction. Then suddenly, with a kind of mental gasp, she remembered Judith Church.

"Ah!" she said to herself, and her lips almost moved. "What a complication!" And then darted up from some depth of her moral consciousness the thought, "She ought to know, and I ought to tell her."

She tried to look calmly at the situation, and analyse the character of her responsibility. She sought for its *pros* and *cons*; she made an effort to range them and to balance them. But, in spite of herself, her mind rejected everything save the memory of the words she had overheard one soft spring night on the verandah at Government House:

"*You ask me if I am not to you what I ought to be to my husband, who is a good man, and who loves me and trusts you.*"

"And trusts you! and trusts you!" Remembering the way her own blood quickened when she heard Judith Church say that, Rhoda made a spiritual bound towards the conviction that she could not shirk opening such deplorably blind eyes and respect herself in future. Then her memory insisted again, and she heard Judith say, with an inflection that precluded all mistake, all self-delusion, all change:

"*But you ask me if I have come to love you, and perhaps in a way you have a right to know; and the truth is better, as you say. And I answer you that I have. I answer you, Yes, it is true; and I know it will always be true.*"

Did that make no difference? And was there not infinitely too much involved for any such casual, rough-handed interference as hers would be?

At that moment she saw that her husband was putting on his hat. His letter to Mrs. Church lay addressed upon the desk, the papers that were to accompany scattered about it, and Doyle was directing the clerk with regard to them.

"You will put all these in a strong cover, Luteef," said he, "and address it as I have addressed that letter. I would like you to take them to the General Post Office yourself, and see that they don't go under-stamped."

"Yessir. All thee papers, sir? And I am to send by letter-post, sir?"

"Yes, certainly. Well, Rhoda? That was a clever bit of trickery, wasn't it? I heard afterwards that the article was quoted in the House, and did Church a lot of damage."

Doyle spoke with the boldness of embarrassment. These two were not in the habit of discussing Ancram; they tolerated him occasionally as an object, but never as a subject. Already he regretted the impulse that put her in possession of these facts. It seemed to his sensitiveness like taking an unfair advantage of a man when he was down, which, considering to what Lewis Ancram had risen, was a foolish and baseless scruple. Rhoda looked at her husband, and hesitated. For an instant she played with the temptation to tell him all she knew, deciding, at the end of the instant, that it would entail too much. Even a reference to that time had come to cost her a good deal.

"I am somehow not surprised," she said, looking down at the letter and paper in her hand. "But—I think it's a pity Mrs. Church doesn't know."

"Poor dear lady! why should she? I am glad she is spared that unnecessary pang. We should all be allowed to think as well of the world as we can, my wife. Come; in twenty minutes it will be dark."

"Do you think so?" his wife asked doubtfully. But she threw the letter and the newspaper upon the desk. She would shirk it; as a duty it was not plain enough.

"Then you ought to burn those, Philip," she said, as they went downstairs together. "They wouldn't make creditable additions to the records of the India Office."

"I will," replied her husband. "I don't know why I didn't long ago. How deliciously fresh it is after the rain!"

CHAPTER XXIII.

THERE was a florist's near by—in London there always is a florist's near by—and Judith stood in the little place, among the fanciful straw baskets and the wire frames and the tin boxes of cut flowers and the damp pots of blooming ones, and made her choice. In her slenderness and her gladness she herself had somewhat the poise of a flower, and the delicate flush of her face, with its new springing secret of life, did more to suggest one—a flower just opened to the summer and the sun.

She picked out some that were growing in country lanes then—it was the middle of July—poppies and cornbottles and big brown-hearted daisies. They seemed to her to speak in a simple way of joy. Then she added a pot of ferns and some clustering growing azaleas, pink and white and very lovely. She paid the florist's wife ten

shillings, and took them all with her in a cab. This was not a day for economies. She drove back to her rooms, the azaleas beside her on the seat making a picture of her that people turned to look at. In her hand she carried a folded brown envelope. On the form inside it was written, in the generically inexpressive characters of the Telegraph Department, "*Arrive London 2.30. Will be with you at five. Ancram.*"

It was ten o'clock in the morning, but she felt that the day would be too short for all there was to do. There should be nothing sordid in her greeting, nothing to make him remember that she was poor. Her attic should be swept and garnished: women think of these little things. She had also with her in the cab a pair of dainty Liberty muslin curtains to keep out the roof and the chimneys, and a Japanese tea-set, and tea of a kind she was not in the habit of drinking. She had only stopped buying pretty fresh decorative things when it occurred to her that she must keep enough money to pay the cabman. As she hung the curtains, and put the ferns on the window-seat and the azaleas in the corners, and the plump, delicate-coloured silk cushions in the angles of her small hard sofa, her old love of soft luxurious things stirred within her. Instinctively she put her poverty away with impatience and contempt. What in another woman might have been a calculating thought came to her as a hardly acknowledged sense of relief and repose. There would be no more of *that!*

A knock at the door sent the blood to her heart, and her hand to her dusty hair, before she remembered how impossible it was that this should be any but an unimportant knock. Yet she opened the door with a thrill—it seemed that such a day could have no trivial incidents. When she saw that it was the housemaid with the mail, the Indian mail, she took it with a little smile of indifference and satisfaction. It was no longer the master of her delight.

She put it all aside while she adjusted the folds of the curtains and took the step-ladder out of the room. Then she read Philip Doyle's letter. She read it, and when she had finished she looked gravely, coldly, at the packet that came with it, carefully addressed in the round accurate hand of the clerk who made quill pens in Doyle's office. She was conscious of an unkindness in this chance; it might so well have fallen last week or next. There was no ignoring it—it was there, it had been delivered to her, it seemed almost as urgent a demand upon her time and thought and interest as if John Church himself had put it into her hand. With an involuntary movement she pushed the packet aside and looked round the room. There were still several little things to do. She got up to go about them; but she moved slowly, and the glow had gone out of her face, leaving her eyes shadowed as they were on other days. She made the cornbottles and the daisies up into little bouquets, but she let her hands drop into her lap more than once, and thought about other things.

Suddenly, with a quick movement, she went over to where the packet lay and took it up.

It was as if she turned her back upon something; she had a resolute look. As she broke the wax and cut the strings, any one might have recognised that she confronted herself with a duty which she did not mean to postpone. It would have been easy to guess her unworded feeling—that, however differently her heart might insist, she could not slight John Church. This was a sensitive and a just woman.

She opened letter after letter, reading slowly and carefully. Every word had its due, every sentence spoke to her. Gradually there came round her lips the look they wore when she knelt upon her hassock in St. Luke's round the corner, and repeated, with bent head,

"But Thou, O Lord, have mercy upon us, miserable offenders:
Spare Thou them, O Lord, which confess their faults."

It seemed to her that in not having loved John Church while he lived nor mourned him in sackcloth when he was dead she had sinned indeed.

She was in the midst of preparations that were almost bridal, yet it is quite true that for this man whose death had wrought her deliverance and her joy, her eyes were full of a tender, reverent regret. Presently she came upon a letter which she put aside, with a pang, to be read last of all. It was like Ancram, she thought, to have borne witness to her husband's worth—he could never have guessed that his letter would hurt her a little one day. She noticed that it was fastened together with a newspaper, by a narrow rubber circlet, and that the newspaper was marked in red pencil. She remembered Ancram's turn for journalism—he had acknowledged many a clever article to her—and divined that this was some tribute from his pen. The idea gave her a realising sense that her lover shared her penance and was vaguely comforting.

She went through all the rest, as I have said, conscientiously, seriously, and with a troubled heart. Philip Doyle had not been mistaken in saying that they were sincere, and spontaneous. The tragedy of Church's death had brought out his motives in high relief; it was not likely he could ever have lived to be so appreciated. These were impressions of him struck off as it were in a white heat of feeling. His widow sat for a moment silent before the revelation they made of him, even to her.

Then, to leave nothing undone, Judith opened Ancram's letter. Her startled eyes went through it once without comprehending a line of its sequence, though here and there words struck her in the face and made it burn. She put her hand to her head to steady herself; she felt giddy, and sickeningly unable to comprehend. She fastened her gaze upon the page, seeing nothing, while her brain worked automatically about the fact that she was the victim of some terribly untoward circumstance —what and why it refused to discover for her. Presently things grew simpler and clearer; she realised the direction from which the blow had come. Her power to reason, to consider, to compare, came back to her; and she caught up her misfortune eagerly, to minimise it. The lines of Ancram's hostility and contempt traced themselves again upon her mind, and this time it quivered under their full significance. "Happily for Bengal," she read, "a fool is invariably dealt with according to his folly." Then she knew that no mollifying process of reasoning could alter the fact which she had to face.

Her mind grew acute in its pain. She began to make deductions, she looked at the date. The corroboration of the newspaper flashed upon her instantly, and with it came a keen longing to tell her husband who had written that article—he had wondered so often and so painfully. All at once she found herself framing a charge.

A clock struck somewhere, and as if the sound summoned her she got up from her seat and opened a little lacquered box that stood upon the mantel. It contained letters chiefly, but from among its few photographs she drew one of her husband. With this in her hand she went into her bedroom and shut the door and locked it.

When the maid brought Sir Lewis Ancram's card up at five o'clock she found the door open. Mrs. Church was fitting a photograph into a little frame. She looked thoughtful, but charming; and she said so unhesitatingly, " Bring the gentleman up, Hetty," that Hetty, noticing the curtains and the cushions in Mrs. Church's sitting-room, brought the gentleman up with a smile.

At his step upon the stair her eyes dilated, she took a long breath and pulled herself together, her hand tightening on the corner of the table. He came in quickly and stood before her silent; he seemed to insist upon his presence and on his outstretched hands. His face was almost open and expansive in its achieved happiness; one would have said he was a fellow-being and not a Lieutenant-Governor. It looked as if to him the moment were emotional, but Mrs. Church almost immediately deprived it of that character. She gave him the right hand of ordinary intercourse and an agreeable smile.

" You are looking surprisingly well," she said.

If this struck Ancram as inadequate he hesitated about saying so. The words upon his own lips were "My God! how glad I am to see you!" but he did not permit these to escape him either. Her friendliness was too cheerful to chill him, but he put his eyeglass into his eye, which he generally did when he wanted to reflect, behind a pause.

"And you are just the same," he said. "A little more colour, perhaps."

"I am not really, you know," she returned, slipping her hand quickly out of his. "Since I saw you I am older—and wiser. Nearly two years older and wiser."

The smile which he sent into her eyes was a visible effort to bring himself nearer to her.

"Where have you found so much instruction?" he asked, with tender banter.

Her laugh accepted the banter and ignored its quality. "In 'The Modern Influence of the Vedic Books,' among other places," she said, and rang the bell. "Tea, Hetty."

"I must be allowed to congratulate you upon that," she went on pleasantly. "All the wise people are talking about it, aren't they? And upon the rest of your achievements. They have been very remarkable."

"They are very incomplete," he hinted; "but I am glad you are disposed to be kind about them."

They had dropped into chairs at the usual conversational distance, and he sat regarding her with a look which almost confessed that he did not understand.

"I suppose you had an execrable passage," Judith volunteered, with sociable emphasis. "I can imagine what it must have been, as far as Aden, with the monsoon well on."

"Execrable," he repeated. He had come to a conclusion. It was part of her moral conception of their situation that he should begin his love-making over again. She would not tolerate their picking it up and going on with it. At least that was her attitude. He wondered, indulgently, how long she would be able to keep it.

"And Calcutta? I suppose you left it steaming?"

"I hardly know. I was there only a couple of days before the mail left. Almost the whole of July I have been on tour."

"Oh—really?" said Mrs. Church. Her face assumed the slight sad impenetrability with which we give people to understand that they are trespassing upon ground hallowed by the association of grief. Ancram observed, with irritation, that she almost imposed silence upon him for a moment. Her look suggested to him that if he made any further careless allusions she might break into tears.

"Dear me!" Judith said softly at last, pouring out the tea, "how you bring everything back to me!"

He thought of saying boldly that he had come to bring her back to everything, but for some reason he refrained.

"Not unpleasantly, I hope?" He had an instant's astonishment at finding such a commonplace upon his lips. He had thought of this in poems for months.

She gave him his tea, and a pathetic smile. It was so pathetic that he looked away from it, and his eye fell upon the portrait of John Church, framed, near her on the table.

"Do you think it is a good one?" she asked eagerly, following his glance. "Do you think it does him justice? It was so difficult," she added softly, "to do him justice."

Sir Lewis Ancram stirred his tea vigorously. He never took sugar, but the manipulation of his spoon enabled him to say, with candid emphasis, "He never got justice."

For the moment he would abandon his personal interest, he would humour her conscience; he would dwell upon the past, for the moment.

"No," she said, "I think he never did. Perhaps, now——"

Ancram's lip curled expressively.

"Yes, now," he said—"now that no appreciation can encourage him, no applause stimulate him, now that he is for ever past it and them, they can find nothing too good to say of him. What a set of curs they are!"

"It is the old story," she replied. Her eyes were full of sadness.

"Forgive me!" Ancram said involuntarily. Then he wondered for what he had asked to be forgiven.

"He was a martyr," Judith went on calmly— "'John Church, martyr,' is the way they ought to write him down in the Service records. But there were a few people who knew him great and worthy while he lived. I was one——"

"And I was another. There were more than you think."

"He used to trust you. Especially in the matter that killed him—that educational matter —he often said that without your sympathy and support he would hardly know where to turn."

"His policy was right. Events are showing now how right it was. Every day I find what excellent reason he had for all he did."

"Yes," Judith said, regarding him with a kind of remote curiosity. "You have succeeded to his difficulties. I wonder if you lie awake over them, as he used to do! And to all the rest.

You have taken his place, and his hopes, and the honours that would have been his. How strange it seems!"

"Why should it seem so strange, Judith?"

She half turned and picked up a letter and a newspaper that lay on the table behind her.

"This is one reason," she said, and handed them to him. "Those have reached me to-day, by some mistake in Mr. Doyle's office, I suppose. One knows how these things happen in India. And I thought you might like to have them again."

Ancram's face fell suddenly into the lines of office. He took the papers into his long nervous hands in an accustomed way, and opened the pages of the letter with a stroke of his finger and thumb which told of a multitude of correspondence and a somewhat disregarding way of dealing with it. His eyes were riveted upon Doyle's red pencil marks under "*his beard grows with the tale of his blunders*" in the letter and the newspaper, but his expression merely noted them for future reference.

"Thanks," he said presently, settling the

papers together again. "Perhaps it is as well that they should be in my possession. It was thoughtful of you. In other hands they might be misunderstood."

She looked at him full and clearly, and something behind her eyes laughed at him.

"Oh, I think not!" she said. "Let me give you another cup of tea."

"No more, thank you." He drew his feet together in a preliminary movement of departure, and then thought better of it.

"I hope you understand," he said, "that in— in official life one may be forced into hostile criticism occasionally, without the slightest personal animus." His voice was almost severe—it was as he were compelled to reason with a subordinate in terms of reproof.

Judith smiled acquiescently.

"Oh, I am sure that must often be the case," she said; and he knew that she was beyond all argument of his. She had adopted the official attitude; she was impersonal and complaisant and non-committal. Her comment would reach him later, through the authorised channels of the empty years. It would be silent and negative in its nature, the denial of promotion, but he would understand. Even in a matter of sentiment the official attitude had its decencies, its conveniences. He was vaguely aware of them as he rose, with a little cough, and fell back into his own.

Nevertheless it was with something like an inward groan that he abandoned it, and tried, for a few lingering minutes, to remind her of the man she had known in Calcutta.

"Judith," he said desperately at the door, after she had bidden him a cheerful farewell, "I once thought I had reason to believe that you loved me."

She was leaning rather heavily on the back of a chair. He had made only a short visit, but he had spent five years of this woman's life since he arrived.

"Not you," she said: "my idea of you. And that was a long time ago."

She kept her tone of polite commonplace; there was nothing for it but a recognisant bow, which Ancram made in silence. As he took his way downstairs and out into Kensington, a malignant recollection of having heard something very like this before took possession of him and interfered with the heroic quality of his grief. If he had a Nemesis, he told himself, it was the feminine idea of him. But that was afterward.

. . . .

One day, a year later, Sir Lewis Ancram paused in his successful conduct of the affairs of Bengal long enough to state the case with ultimate emphasis to a confidentially inquiring friend.

"As the wife of my late honoured chief," he said, "I have the highest admiration and respect for Mrs. Church; but the world is wrong in thinking that I have ever made her a proposal of marriage; nor have I the slightest intention of doing so."

THE END.

D. APPLETON & CO.'S PUBLICATIONS.

BY S. R. CROCKETT.

CLEG KELLY, ARAB OF THE CITY. His *Progress and Adventures.* Uniform with "The Lilac Sunbonnet" and "Bog-Myrtle and Peat." Illustrated. 12mo. Cloth, $1.50.

It is safe to predict for the quaint and delightful figure of Cleg Kelly a notable place in the literature of the day. Mr. Crockett's signal success in his new field will enlarge the wide circle of his admirers. The lights and shadows of curious phases of Edinburgh life, and of Scotch farm and railroad life, are pictured with an intimate sympathy, richness of humor, and truthful pathos which make this new novel a genuine addition to literature. It seems safe to say that at least two characters—Cleg and Muckle Alick—are likely to lead Mr. Crockett's heroes in popular favor. The illustrations of this fascinating novel have been the result of most faithful and sympathetic study.

BOG-MYRTLE AND PEAT. Third edition. 12mo. Cloth, $1.50.

"Here are idyls, epics, dramas of human life, written in words that thrill and burn. . . . Each is a poem that has an immortal flavor. They are fragments of the author's early dreams, too bright, too gorgeous, too full of the blood of rubies and the life of diamonds to be caught and held palpitating in expression's grasp."—*Boston Courier.*

"Hardly a sketch among them all that will not afford pleasure to the reader for its genial humor, artistic local coloring, and admirable portrayal of character."—*Boston Home Journal.*

"One dips into the book anywhere and reads on and on, fascinated by the writer's charm of manner."—*Minneapolis Tribune.*

THE LILAC SUNBONNET. Sixth edition. 12mo. Cloth, $1.50.

"A love story pure and simple, one of the old-fashioned, wholesome, sunshiny kind, with a pure-minded, sound-hearted hero, and a heroine who is merely a good and beautiful woman; and if any other love story half so sweet has been written this year, it has escaped our notice."—*New York Times.*

"The general conception of the story, the motive of which is the growth of love between the young chief and heroine, is delineated with a sweetness and a freshness, a naturalness and a certainty, which places 'The Lilac Sunbonnet' among the best stories of the time."—*New York Mail and Express.*

"In its own line this little love story can hardly be excelled. It is a pastoral, an idyl—the story of love and courtship and marriage of a fine young man and a lovely girl—no more. But it is told in so thoroughly delightful a manner, with such playful humor, such delicate fancy, such true and sympathetic feeling, that nothing more could be desired."—*Boston Traveller.*

New York: D. APPLETON & CO., 72 Fifth Avenue.

D. APPLETON & CO.'S PUBLICATIONS.

By A. CONAN DOYLE.

THE EXPLOITS OF BRIGADIER GERARD. A Romance of the *Life* of *a* Typical Napoleonic Soldier. Illustrated. 12mo. Cloth, $1.50.

There is a flavor of Dumas's Musketeers in the life of the redoubtable **Brigadier Gerard**, a typical Napoleonic soldier, more fortunate than many of his **compeers because** some of his Homeric exploits were accomplished under **the personal observation of the Emperor.** His delightfully romantic career included **an oddly characteristic glimpse** of England, and his adventures ranged from the **battlefield to secret service.** In picturing the experiences of his fearless, **hard fighting and hard-drinking hero, the author** of "The White Company" **has given us a book which absorbs the interest and** quickens the pulse of every reader.

THE STARK MUNRO LETTERS. Being a Series of Twelve Letters written by STARK MUNRO, M. B., to his friend and former fellow-student, Herbert Swanborough, of Lowell, Massachusetts, during the years 1881–1884. Illustrated. 12mo. Buckram, $1.50.

"Cullingworth, . . . a much more interesting creation than Sherlock Holmes, and I pray Dr. Doyle to give us more of him."—*Richard le Gallienne, in the London Star.*

"Every one who wants a hearty laugh must make acquaintance with Dr. James Cullingworth."—*Westminster Gazette.*

"Every one must read; for not to know Cullingworth should surely argue one's self to be unknown."—*Pall Mall Gazette.*

"One of the freshest figures to be met with in any recent fiction."—*London Daily News.*

"'The Stark Munro Letters' is a bit of real literature. . . . Its reading will be an epoch-making event in many a life."—*Philadelphia Evening Telegraph.*

"Positively magnetic, and written with that combined force and grace for which the author's style is known."—*Boston Budget.*

SEVENTH EDITION.

ROUND THE RED LAMP. Being Facts and Fancies of Medical Life. 12mo. Cloth, $1.50.

"Too much can not be said in praise of these strong productions, that, to read, keep one's heart leaping to the throat and the mind in a tumult of anticipation to the end. . . . No series of short stories in modern literature can approach them."—*Hartford Times.*

"If Mr. A. Conan Doyle had not already placed himself in the front rank of living English writers by 'The Refugees,' and other of his larger stories, he would surely do so by these fifteen short tales."—*New York Mail and Express.*

"A strikingly realistic and decidedly original contribution to modern literature."—*Boston Saturday Evening Gazette.*

New York: D. APPLETON & CO., 72 Fifth Avenue.

D. APPLETON & CO.'S PUBLICATIONS.

THE ONE WHO LOOKED ON. By F. F. MONTRÉSOR, author of "Into the Highways and Hedges." 16mo. Cloth, special binding, $1.25.

"The story runs on as smoothly as a brook through lowlands; it excites your interest at the beginning and keeps it to the end."—*New York Herald.*

"An exquisite story. . . . No person sensitive to the influence of what makes for the true, the lovely, and the strong in human friendship and the real in life's work can read this book without being benefited by it."—*Buffalo Commercial.*

"The book has universal interest and very unusual merit. . . . Aside from its subtle poetic charm, the book is a noble example of the power of keen observation."—*Boston Herald.*

CORRUPTION. By PERCY WHITE, author of "Mr. Bailey-Martin," etc. 12mo. Cloth, $1.25.

"There is intrigue enough in it for those who love a story of the ordinary kind, and the political part is perhaps more attractive in its sparkle and variety of incident than the real thing itself."—*London Daily News.*

"A drama of biting intensity, a tragedy of inflexible purpose and relentless result."—*Pall Mall Gazette.*

A HARD WOMAN. A Story in Scenes. By VIOLET HUNT. 12mo. Cloth, $1.25.

"An extremely clever work. Miss Hunt probably writes dialogue better than any of our young novelists. . . . Not only are her conversations wonderfully vivacious and sustained, but she contrives to assign to each of her characters a distinct mode of speech, so that the reader easily identifies them, and can follow the conversations without the slightest difficulty."—*London Athenæum.*

"One of the best writers of dialogue of our immediate day. The conversations in this book will enhance her already secure reputation."—*London Daily Chronicle.*

"A creation that does Miss Hunt infinite credit, and places her in the front rank of the younger novelists. . . . Brilliantly drawn, quivering with life, adroit, quiet-witted, unfalteringly insolent, and withal strangely magnetic."—*London Standard.*

AN IMAGINATIVE MAN. By ROBERT S. HICHENS, author of "The Green Carnation." 12mo. Cloth, $1.25.

"One of the brightest books of the year."—*Boston Budget.*

"Altogether delightful, fascinating, unusual."—*Cleveland Amusement Gazette.*

"A study in character. . . . Just as entertaining as though it were the conventional story of love and marriage. The clever hand of the author of 'The Green Carnation' is easily detected in the caustic wit and pointed epigram."—*Jeannette L. Gilder, in the New York World.*

New York: D. APPLETON & CO., 72 Fifth Avenue.

D. APPLETON & CO.,'S PUBLICATIONS.

"A better book than 'The Prisoner of Zenda.'"—*London Queen.*

THE CHRONICLES OF COUNT ANTONIO. By ANTHONY HOPE, author of "The God in the Car," "The Prisoner of Zenda," etc. With photogravure Frontispiece by S. W. Van Schaick. Third edition. 12mo. Cloth, $1.50.

"No adventures were ever better worth recounting than are those of Antonio of Monte Velluto, a very Bayard among outlaws. . . . To all those whose pulses still stir at the recital of deeds of high courage, we may recommend this book. . . . The chronicle conveys the emotion of heroic adventure, and is picturesquely written."—*London Daily News.*

"It has literary merits all its own, of a deliberate and rather deep order. . . . In point of execution 'The Chronicles of Count Antonio' is the best work that Mr. Hope has yet done. The design is clearer, the workmanship more elaborate, the style more colored. . . . The incidents are most ingenious, they are told quietly, but with great cunning, and the Quixotic sentiment which pervades it all is exceedingly pleasant."—*Westminster Gazette.*

"A romance worthy of all the expectations raised by the brilliancy of his former books, and likely to be read with a keen enjoyment and a healthy exaltation of the spirits by every one who takes it up."—*The Scotsman.*

"A gallant tale, written with unfailing freshness and spirit."—*London Daily Telegraph.*

"One of the most fascinating romances written in English within many days. The quaint simplicity of its style is delightful, and the adventures recorded in these 'Chronicles of Count Antonio' are as stirring and ingenious as any conceived even by Weyman at his best."—*New York World.*

"Romance of the real flavor, wholly and entirely romance, and narrated in true romantic style. The characters, drawn with such masterly handling, are not merely pictures and portraits, but statues that are alive and step boldly forward from the canvas."—*Boston Courier.*

"Told in a wonderfully simple and direct style, and with the magic touch of a man who has the genius of narrative, making the varied incidents flow naturally and rapidly in a stream of sparkling discourse."—*Detroit Tribune.*

"Easily ranks with, if not above, 'A Prisoner of Zenda.' . . . Wonderfully strong, graphic, and compels the interest of the most *blasé* novel reader."—*Boston Advertiser.*

"No adventures were ever better worth telling than those of Count Antonio. . . . The author knows full well how to make every pulse thrill, and how to hold his readers under the spell of his magic."—*Boston Herald.*

"A book to make women weep proud tears, and the blood of men to tingle with knightly fervor. . . . In 'Count Antonio' we think Mr. Hope surpasses himself, as he has already surpassed all the other story-tellers of the period."—*New York Spirit of the Times.*

New York: D. APPLETON & CO., 72 Fifth Avenue.

D. APPLETON & CO.'S PUBLICATIONS.

THE REDS OF THE MIDI. An Episode of the French Revolution. By FÉLIX GRAS. Translated from the Provençal by Mrs. CATHARINE A. JANVIER. With an Introduction by THOMAS A. JANVIER. With Frontispiece. 12mo. Cloth, $1.50.

M. Félix Gras is the official head of the *Félibrige*, the society of Provençal men of letters, the highest honor in their gift. It is believed that the introduction of his rare talent to our readers will meet with prompt appreciation.

"In all French history there is no more inspiring episode than that with which M. Gras deals in this story: the march to Paris and the doings in Paris of that Marseilles Battalion made up of men who were sworn to cast down 'the tyrant,' and who 'knew how to die.' His epitome of the motive power of the Revolution in the feelings of one of its individual pleasant parts is the very essence of simplicity and directness. His method has the largeness and clearness of the Greek drama. The motives are distinct. The action is free and bold. The climax is inevitable, and the story has a place entirely apart from all the fiction of the French Revolution with which I am acquainted."—*From Mr. Janvier's Introduction.*

THE GODS, SOME MORTALS, AND LORD WICKENHAM. By JOHN OLIVER HOBBES. With Portrait. 12mo. Cloth, $1.50.

"Mrs. Craigie has taken her place among the novelists of the day. It is a high place and a place apart. Her method is her own, and she stands not exactly on the threshold of a great career, but already within the temple of fame."—*G. W. Smalley, in the Tribune.*

"Here is the sweetness of a live love story. . . . It is to be reckoned among the brilliants as a novel."—*Boston Courier.*

"One of the most refreshing novels of the period, full of grace, spirit, force, feeling, and literary charm."—*Chicago Evening Post.*

"Clever and cynical, full of epigrams and wit, bright with keen delineations of character, and with a shrewd insight into life."—*Newark Advertiser.*

"A novel of profound psychological knowledge and ethical import. . . . Worthy of high rank in current fiction."—*Boston Beacon.*

MAELCHO. By the Hon. EMILY LAWLESS, author of "Grania," "Hurrish," etc. 12mo. Cloth, $1.50.

"A paradox of literary genius. It is not a history, and yet has more of the stuff of history in it, more of the true national character and fate, than any historical monograph we know. It is not a novel, and yet fascinates us more than any novel."—*London Spectator.*

"Abounds in thrilling incidents. . . . Above and beyond all, the book charms by reason of the breadth of view, the magnanimity, and the tenderness which animate the author."—*London Athenæum.*

"A piece of work of the first order, which we do not hesitate to describe as one of the most remarkable literary achievements of this generation."—*Manchester Guardian.*

New York: D. APPLETON & CO., 72 Fifth Avenue.

D. APPLETON & CO.'S PUBLICATIONS.

SLEEPING FIRES. By GEORGE GISSING, author of "In the Year of Jubilee," "Eve's Ransom," etc. 16mo. Cloth, 75 cents.

In this striking story the author has treated an original motive with rare self-command and skill. His book is most interesting as a story, and remarkable as a literary performance.

STONEPASTURES. By ELEANOR STUART. 16mo. Cloth, 75 cents.

"This is a strong bit of good literary workmanship. . . . The book has the value of being a real sketch of our own mining regions, and of showing how, even in the apparently dull round of work, there is still material for a good bit of literature."—*Philadelphia Ledger.*

COURTSHIP BY COMMAND. By M. M. BLAKE. 16mo. Cloth, 75 cents.

"A bright, moving study of an unusually interesting period in the life of Napoleon, . . . deliciously told; the characters are clearly, strongly, and very delicately modeled, and the touches of color most artistically done. 'Courtship by Command' is the most satisfactory Napoleon *bonne-bouche* we have had."—*New York Commercial Advertiser.*

THE WATTER'S MOU'. By BRAM STOKER. 16mo. Cloth, 75 cents.

"Here is a tale to stir the most sluggish nature. . . . It is like standing on the deck of a wave-tossed ship; you feel the soul of the storm go into your blood."—*N. Y. Home Journal.*

"The characters are strongly drawn, the descriptions are intensely dramatic, and the situations are portrayed with rare vividness of language. It is a thrilling story, told with great power."—*Boston Advertiser.*

MASTER AND MAN. By Count LEO TOLSTOY. With an Introduction by W. D. HOWELLS. 16mo. Cloth, 75 cents.

"Crowded with these characteristic touches which mark his literary work."—*Public Opinion.*

"Reveals a wonderful knowledge of the workings of the human mind, and it tells a tale that not only stirs the emotions, but gives us a better insight into our own hearts."—*San Francisco Argonaut.*

THE ZEIT-GEIST. By L. DOUGALL, author of "The Mermaid," "Beggars All," etc. 16mo. Cloth, 75 cents.

"One of the best of the short stories of the day."—*Boston Journal.*

"One of the most remarkable novels of the year."—*New York Commercial Advertiser.*

"Powerful in conception, treatment, and influence."—*Boston Globe.*

New York: D. APPLETON & CO., 72 Fifth Avenue.

D. APPLETON & CO.'S PUBLICATIONS.

TWO REMARKABLE AMERICAN NOVELS.

THE RED BADGE OF COURAGE. An Episode of the American Civil War. By STEPHEN CRANE. 12mo. Cloth, $1.00.

"Mr. Stephen Crane is a great artist, with something new to say, and consequently with a new way of saying it. . . . In 'The Red Badge of Courage' Mr. Crane has surely contrived a masterpiece. . . . He has painted a picture that challenges comparisons with the most vivid scenes of Tolstoy's 'La Guerre et la Paix' or of Zola's 'La Débâcle.'"—*London New Review.*

"In its whole range of literature we can call to mind nothing so searching in its analysis, so manifestly impressed with the stamp of truth, as 'The Red Badge of Courage.' . . . A remarkable study of the average mind under stress of battle. . . . We repeat, a really fine achievement."—*London Daily Chronicle.*

"Not merely a remarkable book; it is a revelation. . . . One feels that, with perhaps one or two exceptions, all previous descriptions of modern warfare have been the merest abstractions."—*St. James Gazette.*

"Holds one irrevocably. There is no possibility of resistance when once you are in its grip, from the first of the march of the troops to the closing scenes. . . . Mr. Crane, we repeat, has written a remarkable book. His insight and his power of realization amount to genius."—*Pall Mall Gazette.*

"There is nothing in American fiction to compare with it in the vivid, uncompromising, almost aggressive vigor with which it depicts the strangely mingled conditions that go to make up what men call war. . . . Mr. Crane has added to American literature something that has never been done before, and that is, in its own peculiar way, inimitable."—*Boston Beacon.*

"Never before have we had the seamy side of glorious war so well depicted. . . . The action of the story throughout is splendid, and all aglow with color, movement, and vim. The style is as keen and bright as a sword-blade, and a Kipling has done nothing better in this line."—*Chicago Evening Post.*

IN DEFIANCE OF THE KING. A Romance of the American Revolution. By CHAUNCEY C. HOTCHKISS. 12mo. Paper, 50 cents; cloth, $1.00.

"The whole story is so completely absorbing that you will sit far into the night to finish it. You lay it aside with the feeling that you have seen a gloriously true picture of the Revolution."—*Boston Herald.*

"The story is a strong one—a thrilling one. It causes the true American to flush with excitement, to devour chapter after chapter until the eyes smart; and it fairly smokes with patriotism."—*New York Mail and Express.*

"The heart beats quickly, and we feel ourselves taking part in the scenes described. . . . Altogether the book is an addition to American literature."—*Chicago Evening Post.*

"One of the most readable novels of the year. . . . As a love romance it is charming, while it is filled with thrilling adventure and deeds of patriotic daring."—*Boston Advertiser.*

"This romance seems to come the nearest to a satisfactory treatment in fiction of the Revolutionary period that we have yet had."—*Buffalo Courier.*

"A clean, wholesome story, full of romance and interesting adventure. . . . Holds the interest alike by the thread of the story and by the incidents. . . . A remarkably well-balanced and absorbing novel."—*Milwaukee Journal.*

New York: D. APPLETON & CO., 72 Fifth Avenue.

www.ingramcontent.com/pod-product-compliance
Lightning Source LLC
Chambersburg PA
CBHW031851220426
43663CB00006B/584